Noah Porter

An Historical Discourse Delivered at the Celebration of the 100th Anniversary of the Erection of the Congregational Church in Farmington

Noah Porter

An Historical Discourse Delivered at the Celebration of the 100th Anniversary of the Erection of the Congregational Church in Farmington

ISBN/EAN: 9783337235956

Printed in Europe, USA, Canada, Australia, Japan

Cover: Foto ©ninafisch / pixelio.de

More available books at **www.hansebooks.com**

AN HISTORICAL DISCOURSE

DELIVERED AT THE

Celebration of the One Hundredth Anniversary

OF THE ERECTION OF THE

CONGREGATIONAL CHURCH

IN

FARMINGTON, CONN.

October 16, 1872.

By NOAH PORTER. D. D

PRESIDENT OF YALE COLLEGE.

HARTFORD:
CASE, LOCKWOOD & BRAINARD, PRINTERS.
1873.

PREFACE.

At a special meeting of the First Ecclesiastical Society of Farmington, held May 5th, 1871, it was voted "that a committee of five be appointed to devise ways and means to have a proper celebration of the one hundredth anniversary of the building of our church in this village; and Julius Gay, Edward Norton, John S. Rice, Thomas Cowles, and Samuel S. Cowles were appointed said committee."

The committee met accordingly, and, having in mind the address of President Porter, to which many of us had listened, on a somewhat similar occasion thirty years before, with no ordinary interest, we deemed it most fitting that he who had worshiped in the old church in his boyhood, and whose venerated sire had so faithfully and so well for sixty years ministered to this people, should again meet with us and rehearse the story of these hundred years.

After an examination of the records of the Society, it appeared that the inscription, "July, 1771," cut upon the foundation stones of the building, had reference only to that portion of the structure, while the remainder of the house was not finished until the year following and the "Dedication Lecture" was preached on the 25th of November, 1772. It was therefore decided that the commemoration exercises should be held as nearly upon the one hundredth anniversary of the dedication as the coolness of the season rendered desirable. The following circular was sent far and wide to all the old residents, whose address could be ascertained:

"One hundred years having passed since the erection of the present church edifice, at Farmington, Conn., it is proposed to hold commemorative services Wednesday, October 16th, 1872, at half-past ten o'clock, A. M.

The Committee are happy to announce that, with other appropriate exercises, there will be an Historical Address by President PORTER, of Yale College.

It would add much to the interest of the occasion should there be present a large representation of those who have gone out from us, also of others, who with no personal associations, may yet be interested in the growth and prosperity of this ancient church of Christ.

To all such, a most cordial invitation is extended to unite with us in the celebration of this anniversary.

In cases where an acceptance of this invitation is impossible, letters, embodying interesting facts and reminiscences, will be gratefully received.

Persons residing at a distance, who propose to be present, will confer a favor on the Committee by sending in their names at an early date, in order that suitable provision may be made.

Early morning trains from New Haven, Northampton, and Hartford arrive at Farmington Station at 8.08, A. M., and evening trains leave said station for either of those places at 7 P. M.

JULIUS GAY,
JOHN S. RICE,
SAMUEL S. COWLES, } COMMITTEE.
EDWARD NORTON,
THOMAS COWLES.

FARMINGTON, October 1st, 1872."

The 16th of October was a pleasant day. The church was crowded. The pulpit, the communion table, and the adjacent walls, were covered with floral decorations, amid which appeared the names of the former pastors of the church and of the building committee, and the text: "One Generation passeth away and another Generation cometh." By the side of the pulpit were exhibited the drum by means of which the people were formerly summoned to church on the Sabbath, and some of the carpenters' tools which were used in the construction of the building. After the delivery of the address, the audience was invited to partake of a collation prepared by the ladies of the church.

The exercises in the morning were as follows:

1. VOLUNTARY. "The Lord is in His Holy Temple."
2. INVOCATION.
3. READING OF THE SCRIPTURES. by Rev. J. F. Merriam.

4. ANTHEM.

"And will the great eternal God
On earth establish his abode,
And will He, from His radiant throne
Avow our temples as His own?

These walls our fathers here did raise;
Long may they echo to Thy praise,
And Thou, descending, fill the place
With choicest tokens of Thy grace.

Here let the great Redeemer reign,
With all the glories of His train;
Whilst power divine His word attends,
To conquer foes, and cheer His friends.

Great King of Glory come,
And with Thy favor crown
This temple as Thy dome,
This people as Thy own."

5. PRAYER, by Rev. C. L. Goodell, D. D.

6. ANTHEM.

"Great God, we come with grateful
[hearts,
For blessings which Thy love imparts,
And offer thanks to Thee.

From Thy celestial courts above,
O, smile upon us, God of love.
Let Mercy, with protecting wing,
To contrite hearts forgiveness bring.

Thy goodness smiles on all around,
The blooming mead, the fertile ground,
All speak of love divine.

In every star which decks the sky,
The sun, the moon uplifted high,
We see Thy goodness shine.

These years with blessings Thou hast
[crowned,
In peace and plenty we abound,
While mercies still increase.

In loud thanksgiving let us sing,
And our united offerings bring:
Thy blessings never cease.

And when on earth no more we raise
Our hearts to Thee in prayer and praise,
O may we sing in Heaven!

And there in strains which Angels tell,
The loud thanksgiving anthem swell
For all Thy favors given."

7. HISTORICAL DISCOURSE, by President Noah Porter, D. D.

8. HYMN. Tune "Marlow." Sung by the Congregation.

"O God, our help in ages past,
Our hope for years to come,
Our shelter from the stormy blast,
And our eternal home!

Before the hills in order stood,
Or earth received her frame,
From everlasting Thou art God,
To endless years the same.

A thousand ages, in Thy sight,
Are like an evening gone—

Short as the watch that ends the night
Before the rising sun.

Time, like an ever rolling stream,
Bears all its sons away;
They fly, forgotten, as a dream
Dies at the opening day.

O God! our help in ages past,
Our hope for years to come,
Be Thou our guide while troubles last,
And our eternal home."

9. BENEDICTION.

The afternoon was devoted to short addresses appropriate to the occasion, and remarks were offered by Rev. J. F. Merriam, the pastor of the church, Rev. Seth Bliss, of Berlin, Elihu Burritt, Esq., Gen. Joseph R. Hawley, Hon. Francis Gillette, Rev. J. R. Keep. R. G. Vermilye, D. D., F. Hawley, Esq., Leverett Griggs, D. D., Rev. T. K. Fessenden, Rev. C. L. Goodell, D. D., Dr. Isaac G. Porter.

HISTORICAL DISCOURSE.

This edifice has been used as a place for public worship almost a hundred years. The " Dedication Lecture " was preached Nov. 25th. 1772, and on " the Sabbath " following the congregation began to occupy this house as their place of worship.

A hundred years, when viewed in one aspect, is a brief period and of little consequence ; viewed in another, it is comparatively long, and may be most important in the events which it includes and the influences which it has seen spring into life. It is not nineteen centuries since the Christian era began. The last three or four hundred years of this era have been distinguished as the most eventful of these nineteen, and among these none has witnessed changes so significant and so much for the better as the very last.

It seems scarcely credible that the world of thought and feeling could be what we know it was when this old church was new; that the manners and institutions, the opinions and principles, the inner life and the outward civilization of Christendom have undergone such marvelous changes, while this house has been standing here and looking out upon the stream of progress that has rushed so swiftly by.

As we enter it to-day to honor its fresh and green old age, we are almost impelled to regard it as a living person, and reverently and lovingly to question it concerning the past which it has watched in the busy days, and thought of in the silent nights, during the long years in which it has been keeping sentry on this hill-side. Or, if the fiction be too bold which makes it a person, surely that is not too daring which believes it to be filled at this hour with the spirits of the departed, whose feet have trod in these aisles, whose eyes have looked familiarly upon these walls, and whose instructed minds and reverent hearts have interpreted the course of events, both public and private, local and national, in the light of the divine purposes and the promised redemption of man. It is as one awed and elevated by their presence that I would speak—with faithful truth. yet with affectionate interest in the past history of the community which for a century has known and honored this as the house of God.

First, as is appropriate, I would speak of the edifice and its construction. The first recorded movement towards the erection of this building was on Feb. 2d, 1767, when, at a meeting of the parish, 54 voted, 24 being in the negative, that it was necessary to build a meeting-house in the first society* of Farmington, and Solomon Whitman was directed to apply to the county court to fix the site for the edifice.

Nothing further seems to have been done before December 21st, when it was voted " that a judicious committee should be called to give their opinion whether it was expedient to build a new, or repair the old, structure." Dec. 30th, three builders, probably residing in the neighboring parishes, were selected as this committee. They reported in April, 17 8, that the old meeting-house was not worth repairing.

It was not, however, till February 6th, 1769, that the decisive vote was taken (53 against 12) to build this church. Another agent, Mr. John Strong, was selected to apply to the county court to fix the place, it being stipulated that it

---

* The old town of Farmington at that time consisted of six societies: the first; the second, Great Swamp, 1708, named in 1722 Kensington; the third, Southington, 1722; the fourth, New Cambridge, now Bristol, 1744; the fifth, New Britain, 1754; the sixth, Northington, now Avon, 1750, subsequently divided into East and West Avon. Since the erection of this church edifice, three other Congregational societies have been constituted within the limits of the First Society, viz.: West Britain or Burlington, 1774, Plainville, and Unionville, 1839.

should be within this plot of ground. One penny in a pound
was voted to procure timber; and Capt. Judah Woodruff
and Mr. Fisher Gay were chosen a committee "to procure
thick stuff for the building." Hezekiah Wadsworth and
Isaac Bidwell were subsequently added (Dec. 18th, 1769,) to
these two.

In Dec., 1770, the movements became earnest and decisive.
It was resolved that the timber should be cut that winter,
that the house should be seventy-five feet long and fifty
in breadth, and that it should be framed and set up the
following spring or "fore part of summer." That this was
done is evident from the inscription on the foundation, "July,
1771." The important provisions were added that it should
have a steeple at one end, and a porch at the other for the
stairs leading into the gallery. Both these directions are
somewhat significant.*

In April, 1771, the question of the location came up, and it
was voted, 73 to 32, that it should be placed south-east of the
old house, facing to the north-west or west. It was also voted
that the steeple should be at the north end of the house,
probably after a careful balancing of the relative strength of
the voters of the north and south parts of the parish, or
perhaps because tradition or æsthetic feeling required that a
church situated near the meridian line should look to the
north. Also that there should be "two tiers of hewed stone
foreside of said house, and two-thirds of the way at each
end." At the same meeting, the precise place of the house
was determined by a large committee and approved by the
Society.†

* In all the older, and in many of the later, commodious meeting-houses of
New England, the galleries were reached by stairways within the audience room.
Any person who was ever present in one of these churches and recalls the
stunning and irreverent din made by the youth as they rushed down these noisy
staircases, would not need to be referred to the reason given in the vote passed
on a like occasion at Wethersfield (1760), viz.: "That there shall be a porch
opposite the steeple," and "that stairs be made to go into the galleries in said
steeple and porch and not in the body of said house, that the congregation may
not be interrupted by such as go into the galleries in time of worship, and that
there may be more room in said house."

† The following month this matter was again called up by the committee who
had been appointed by the General Assembly, and 55 voted for the north place,

A number of men were selected from the north and south parts of the Society to aid on alternate days in raising the frame till it should be finished.* It was voted to cover it that summer. In September, it was voted to cover the decking of the steeple with sheet lead. In December, 1771, it was voted to give £20 to Lieut. Abner Curtiss for hurt and damage sustained at the raising of the frame, and to the widow Merrills, whose husband was killed, £6.† It was also voted to finish the church the following summer. In November, 1772, it was voted to meet in it for regular worship.

The two persons who deserve to be named as active in its construction are Col. Fisher Gay and Captain Judah Woodruff.‡ Mr. Gay was one of the two or three leading merchants

so called, 39 for the site of the old house, and about 7 for that place called " The Green."

* The tradition is, that on each day of the raising a large Indian pudding was boiled in a potash kettle for the dinner of the workmen.

† There is still extant in the original MS. an elegiac poem of some two hundred lines on the death of Mr. Merrills, who was a worthy citizen of the White Oak district, a builder by trade, who had not completed his own house at the time of his death. He fell from the roof, or the frame of the attic floor, being struck by a rafter which sent him headlong to the earth. It was for a long time a tradition among the boys that there might be found in the cellar the blood-stained rock on which he fell.

‡ Col. Fisher Gay was the son of John Gay, Jr., who was born in Dedham, Mass., 1698. He was born in Sharon, Oct. 9, 1733, and graduated at Yale College, 1759. At this time he received from his father an English guinea and his father's blessing. He began his life at Farmington as a school teacher, but after two or three years he started a small mercantile business, which, by his energy and skill, became very considerable. He soon became prominent in public affairs. He was appointed one of the committee of correspondence from the town in 1774, and was a member of the other important committees, as of vigilance, preparation, etc. On hearing of the conflict at Concord and Lexington, he shut up his store at once and marched to Boston at the head of about a hundred volunteers. His commission as Lieutenant Colonel is dated January 23, 1776. His last commission as Colonel bears date June 20, 1776. The brief journal which he kept of his services before Boston is preserved. From this it appears that he reported to General Washington Feb. 6th, and on the 13th was sent for by him and immediately despatched into Rhode Island and Connecticut to purchase powder. On the 18th he reported himself with a number of tons, " to the great satisfaction of the General," but was severely ill from over-exertion. The 4th of March he was ordered with his regiment to act as a part of a covering party to the workmen who were detached to fortify Dorchester heights. The success of this attempt led

of the village, and a public-spirited and intelligent man. In obedience to the vote of 1769, he and Captain Woodruff went to Boston for the timber, which was brought from the then Province of Maine, and was of the choicest quality. Captain Woodruff was the architect and master-builder, and the tools

---

to the evacuation of Boston, and Colonel Gay, with his regiment, with Colonel Leonard, Majors Sproat and Chester, and other officers and their troops, were ordered to march in and take possession of the town, where he continued within, or before the works, till the army before Boston broke up, when his regiment was ordered to New York. On his way he spent two or three days with his family for the last time—being at that time very ill. He grew worse after reaching New York. A part of his command was sent to Long Island, and were in the action which followed the retreat, in which last movement they were distinguished. He died August 22, 1776, and was buried on the day of the battle. His zeal and self-sacrifice were conspicuous. On his sword, which is still preserved, are engraved the words, " Freedom or Death ! "

Judah Woodruff was born about 1720, and was the youngest son of Joseph Woodruff, who descended from Matthew Woodruff, one of the eighty-four proprietors of the town. His house stood near the site of the one owned and occupied by the late Noadiah Woodruff, at the north end of the village. At about the age of forty he served as First Lieutenant in the French war, under a warrant signed by " Thomas Fitch, Esq., Captain General and Governor in Chief in and over his Majesty's English Colony of Connecticut, in New England in America. Given on the twenty-second day of March, in the thirty-second year of the reign of his Majesty George the Second, King of Great Britain, Anno Domini 1759. By his Honor's command, George Wyllys Sec'y." He served through the French war, and was at the battle of Ticonderoga.

After the close of the war, he returned home and commenced building, and during the interval between the French war and the war of the Revolution, built ten houses including his own, and also the church of which he was the architect and master builder. At the opening of the Revolutionary war he entered the army and served as an officer. After the close of the war he built four or five other dwelling-houses in this village, which with the ten previously erected, with one or two exceptions are still standing in excellent repair, and with care would last another century.

He was a man of energy and persevering industry, as was proved by his working at late hours, carving upon the pulpit for the church with his knife, after the labors of the day. He was also a man of taste and close observation, and introduced a style of building which added to the respectability of the dwellings of this village. His carving on the front of the pulpit, representing vines of the English ivy, was greatly admired. He probably received many hints in Boston, which city he visited several times, performing his journeys on horse-back.

Captain Woodruff died at the age of seventy-nine, and retained his vigor of mind until the last, while his physical energies were but little impaired until his last sickness. The Rev'd Timothy Pitkin officiated at his funeral, and bore testimony to his earnest piety.

with which he wrought are many of them preserved to
this day. He died in 1799, aged 79, having been about 50
when the church was built. It is surprising that so good
work could have been wrought with so few and such rude appliances. To his skill and thoroughness the village is indebted for many of its most substantial dwellings.* These
houses mark an era in the architecture of the village, and their
workmanship is in striking contrast with that of all the older
dwellings. Among these earlier houses two or three classes
are also easily distinguishable, as to their age and style
of construction. Upon this church Captain Woodruff be-
stowed the utmost care—carving out with his knife the capi-
tals on the pulpit and the fine work of the sounding-board,
in which the wondrous green vines were conspicuous, which
were the admiration of other generations. He spared no
labor or care that the materials should be of the best, and
that the work should be most thoroughly done.† We have no

* The dwelling-houses built by Capt. Woodruff are the following: The Solomon
Cowles house facing the road into the south meadow; the John Mix house; the
Samuel Deming house; the Romanta Norton or Martin Cowles house (1785);
the Samuel S. Cowles house (1769), built for Samuel Smith; the north part of the
Thomas Smith house; the Major Hooker house; the William L. Cowles house;
Col. Fisher Gay's house (1770); the William Whitman house; the Elijah Lewis
house (1789); the Buck House; the homestead of Noadiah Woodruff.

† The stuff was clear of all knots, and whenever there was occasion to cover or
case any of the posts or girths, a single length of boarding was invariably
selected. The shingles were of white cedar, and remain to this day as they were
originally laid—with the exception that here and there one has been loosened
from its place. This extraordinary covering was painted in 1793, and only then.
The frame is of the heaviest white-oak timber, and is still entirely sound and the
lines of the building are perfectly true. The top of the spire is some 150 feet
high, and the spire itself was completed below and lifted to its place along the
tower. The cost of the house was £1750 12s. 10½d., and was defrayed as follows:

				£	s.	d.
Oct. 1771.	By Rev. Mr. Timothy Pitkin,	-	-	£20	00	00
Dec. "	" the first sixpenny vote,	-	-	352	13	4 1-4
" "	" the second "	-	-	352	13	4 1 4
" "	" the fourpenny vote,	-	-	235	02	9 3-4
" "	" three individuals,	-	-	1	19	00
Nov. 1772.	" a vote of 1s. 1d., -	-	-	748	11	02
	Balance, -	-	-	39	13	2 1-4

Mr. Pitkin's salary at this time was £125, the parsonage land in the meadow,
and twenty-five cords of wood.

information as to where he found the design of the edifice.* We only know that this, like many other of the best churches in New England, has a general resemblance to the Old South Church in Boston, which was erected in 1729–30.† The interior of this house was divided on the ground floor by aisles as at present, except that a row of square pews was placed along the walls on every side, a pew in each corner, with one or two benches by the north and the south doors. An aisle extended from the west door to the pulpit, as at present, another aisle from the south to the north door, the two dividing the body of the house into four blocks, each containing six pews. All these remained unpainted till they were removed in 1836, and in them all not a defect or knot was to be seen.

Looking down upon the middle aisle was the formidable pulpit, with a window behind it. It was reached by a staircase on the north side, and was overhung by a wondrous canopy of wood, with a roof like the dome of a Turkish mosque, attached to the wall behind by some hidden device, which stimulated the speculative inquiries of the boys,

---

* It resembles very closely the brick church in Wethersfield which was erected ten years earlier—differing chiefly in being five feet shorter and two feet narrower, and in having more spacious galleries, especially in front. This last feature is to be accounted for by the greater population through the then widely extended parish. The workmanship of the newer edifice for solidity seems to be superior—though the older church is well preserved and has the advantage over the Farmington church in having been altered later, with one or two important improvements upon the changes made in this.

† Some of the older churches, like the old South of Boston, and the churches in Guilford and Milford, were furnished with a second tier of galleries. But doubtless the fathers had by this time learned by experience that it was sufficiently difficult to enforce order in a single gallery.

The following extract of a letter from Rev. Thomas Ruggles to Rev. Thomas Prince, pastor of the old South Church in Boston, deserves notice here. The letter was dated June 10, 1729: "Old Guilford raised a meeting house June, 1712, 68 feet long and 46 feet wide. A steeple 120 feet high was built at the west end of it in 1726. *This was the first steeple built in the Colony of Connecticut.*" The following is also interesting: "At a meeting of the inhabitants of the old or western parish in Guilford Jan. 19, 1725-6, voted that the belfry and spire of the meeting house in this society shall be built in the fashion and proportion of the belfry and spire of the church at Newport, Rhode Island, so near as the Committee can obtain it to be done."

long before they could comprehend the graver mysteries to
which it was supposed to give resonant emphasis. Along
the front of the pulpit was the deacons' seat* in which sat
two worthies whose saintly dignity shone with added luster
and solemnity on the days of holy communion. On the
right of the pulpit was the minister's pew, and on the left
the pew for those who were widows indeed, in dependence as
well as in loneliness. From this narrow pew there opened a
door beneath the pulpit into a closet, of which it was fabled
that it was reserved by the tything man for boys especially
unruly in behavior. The gallery was surrounded by a row of
pews† with three rows of long benches in front, rising as is
usual above one another.

In the winter of 1825-6 the pews and the long seats in the
gallery were demolished and slips were substituted for them,
with doors for more private and special occupation. In 1836
the pews were removed from the floor, the old pulpit and
sounding-board disappeared, new windows were made with
-blinds, etc., at a cost of some $2,186.70. These repairs were
executed after the designs. and under the direction of Timothy Porter, a well trained and thorough builder, who effected
most of the alterations in the spirit of the original. Much of
the cost of these alterations was defrayed from the last legacy
of Solomon Langdon. The steeple was surmounted by a
gilded crown, which remained sole survivor and witness of
the days of colonial dependence, till the year 1836, when
it was taken down to be regilded but not restored to its
old position. It deserves to be noticed, as marking
progress, that in 1795 the doors leading into the house above
and below were provided with pullies, which made their
presence audible for at least forty years after. In 1810 two
large chandeliers‡ were procured, for singing-meetings at

* A table was attached to the deacons' seat or pew by hinges, which when used
was kept in place by braces of twisted iron of a comely fashion.

† High above all the rest b the two entrances were lifted two pews for those of
the African race who sat in the galleries. Corresponding to these in position
were two seats on the floor below.

‡ These chandeliers were made by the well-remembered tin manufacturer and
dealer, Asa Andrews.

night, — an evening sermon or lecture being scarcely known, — which some few of those present will remember, as not unsightly of their kind, although the kind did not attain the highest conceivable beauty. These were simply urn-shaped blocks of wood painted white, suspended from the ceiling above by long rods of iron—twisted here and there for decoration. The eye of many a boy has followed those rods, with an impression of mystery, as to how they were held in their place. From these central urns several flat strips of iron proceeded, curving downward and upward, holding sockets of tin, to receive their tallow candles on those very rare occasions on which the church was lighted.

It was not till 1824 that stoves were introduced. Previous to this period foot-stoves were the sole substitute, for the filling of which the people from a distance were dependent on the liberal fires which were prepared at the hospitable houses in the vicinity. Many a time have I seen so dignified a person as the aged Governor Treadwell strike his well-booted feet together to elicit some warmth as he came in from the snow, before the morning service began.

The place where this house was erected was known as the *Meeting House Green* as early as 1718, as a new school house was directed to be built upon the place with this designation ; " near where the old chestnut tree stood," which was doubtless one of the noble remnants of the original forest. As early as 1743 a general permission was granted to such farmers as lived at a distance to erect small houses along the fences on either side of this green for their comfort on the Sabbath, or as it was phrased, for " their duds and horses." Two such houses stood on the east line, near the town pound, within the memory of many, as late as 1818 or '20. Repeated encroachments have been made upon this enclosure which have been now and then stoutly resisted. The only record of any early effort to make the place attractive is found in the vote which directs the Committee " to bank up decently the new meeting house." At what time the ever memorable Lombardy poplars were planted which so long surrounded the church and the green, we do not know. We know that they lined the village street and were planted in double rows through the cemetery. In 1806 we find the committee directed to secure the shade trees set out on the green in such manner as they think proper, and also " to erect a railing or posts to hitch horses to." These poplars were planted some eight to ten feet distant from the meeting house and about the same distance from one another in front and rear. A double line attended the walk to the front door. Another row bordered the path along near the village street. I can well remember when the horses attached to wagons and other vehicles were tied during service time along the street on either side in front; also behind at the railing which guarded the sacred poplars. In a hot summer afternoon the stamp and occasional scream of these horses often saluted the ear during sermon-time, while the swaying sprays and flickering leaves of the poplars met the eye through the staring windows. Now and then one or two of the many sturdy hearers—of whom a score might be standing divested of their heavy coats to keep themselves reverently awake after a hot week of harvest work—would go out quietly to adjust some strife among the horses, or to extricate an unlucky steed from a serious entanglement.

The swaying poplars will never be forgotten by those who became familiar with their moving walls of glossy greenery as they guarded the sanctuary. How fickle are human fashions and the tastes which admire them ! In 1818 the Committee were directed to cause the two rows of poplars from the meeting house to the road " to be immediately removed." In 1841 the decree went forth that the line which had struggled for existence so long and doubtfully nearest the church should be removed and disposed of " at their discretion." The green remained only partially inclosed till 1853. The highway ran diagonally across and in every direction about it till that time.

Strange as it may appear, no sheds for horses were erected before 1844, long after the other extensive alterations were effected, although the necessity of providing them was earnestly pressed as early as 1807. There was, however, at the north end of the house beyond the steeple a primitive " horse-block." some 5 or 6 feet long, 3 feet wide and 2 feet high, of native red sandstone, along which many a two horse wagon has driven and hastily received its living freight of sturdy sons and laughing daughters, while the horses were rearing and plunging till they were off in dust and wind and sleet. Where now are all those simple and earnest souls, so many of whom cherished so carefully those words of love and hope from the pulpit, which cheered their ride homeward and soothed and elevated the labors of the following week? The whipping-post must not be forgotten, from which now and then fearful screams in the week-time would penetrate the closed windows of the neighboring school-house and appall the younger children, while the older and more hardened boys looked significantly at the master's rod or ferule.* Chained to the whipping-post were the stocks, in which now and then a drunken vagabond found himself encased, but which in the course of nature decayed, and survived in disgraceful impotence long after their occupation was gone.

But I have lingered longer than I should upon the old building and its surroundings, before considering their relations to this community and its history.

The edifice itself is a memorial full of significance. A building so large as this and so expensive indicates that the community had made important advances in wealth, enterprise, and self-respect. It shows plainly that the barbarism and roughness incident to pioneer life had been outgrown. From 1640 to 1720, 80 years, this town had fronted an almost unbroken forest which extended from the wooded horizon which we see from this slope, westward to the Housatonic and northwestward to Lake George. This was the hunting ground of the Tunxis tribe and the marauding ground of the dreaded Mohawk, who might appear either as the foe of his timid subject, or perchance as his ally for the destruction of the whites. For the first sixty years there was a numerous and not always friendly tribe in a garrison and village almost within musket shot of this church.† At the end of the first century the

---

* In 1827 or '8 a man was whipped on the public green of New Haven.

† Early in 1657 an Indian killed a woman and her maid and fired the house, occasioning the destruction of several buildings. The Indians were forced to deliver up the murderer, who was brought to Hartford and executed "as a butcher fells

Indian boys were nearly as numerous as the white boys of the village. The church erected before this was provided with " guard seats," as they were called, where some 10 to 20 men could be on the lookout near the doors against a sudden assault. The space for these seats was relinquished in 1726 for the erection of pews for 8 families, with the provision that the pews should be surrendered should there be subsequent occasion to mount a guard. Later than this, on some occasion of alarm increased by the presence of strange Indians, the men of the Tunxis tribe were required to present themselves daily at the house of Deacon Lee, and pass in review before his daughter, whom they admired and feared.* It is pleasant to find, in 1751, liberty granted to the Christianized Indians to build themselves a seat in the meeting house in the north-east corner over the stairs.† Relays of men were called for to serve in the two or three desperate wars in which the French and Indians combined for the possession of the northern and western line of posts, and in which victory for the French might bring the tomahawk and the torch into this valley. This town sent its share of men to Ticonderoga, and probably to Louisburg; and in this way it trained, as did all the rest of New England, its experienced veterans and its hardy novices for service in the War of Independence.

an ox."—[*Diary of John Hull. Transactions and Publications of the American Antiquarian Society*, vol. iii., p. 180.]

In 1675 Simsbury, then Massacoe, a frontier settlement to the north, was deserted by its inhabitants—some forty families—and totally burned. So complete was the desolation that the returning settlers found it difficult to discover the places where their effects had been secreted.

* Deacon Lee lived a little distance northward from this church on the west side of the street. The Indian garrison and village extended southward to the point of land at the confluence of the Pequabuc and the Tunxis rivers. It is very easy to perceive the reason why this place was selected as their chief residence. It is not easy to walk along the brow of the hill which overlooks the reservation so long styled the Indian neck, without picturing the rude wigwams scattered along this sunny terrace, with canoes idly floating below on the stream which was filled with shad and salmon, while the deer were abundant in the forest that stretched westward and northward to the Mohawk country.

† From the State Records for 1733, '4 and '6, appropriations are ordered from the public treasury for " dieting of the Indian lads at 4 shillings per week for the time they attend the school in said town." In 1734, £33 6s. were paid; in 1736, £28.

3

What this community had been from 1700 and onward, and what it had now become could not be better symbolized than by the old church edifice which was commenced in 1709, completed in 1714, as contrasted with this very carefully constructed and expensive church in 1772. The older—the second church was fifty feet square, with height proportional, and furnished with a cupola or turret which tradition has always placed in the centre, from which the bell rope was suspended so soon as a bell was provided. That this tradition was correct is rendered nearly certain by the existence of churches of a similar form at that period. The church in Hingham, the oldest standing in New England, was built in 1680. It is 55 by 45, the posts being 20 feet high. The cupola rises from the middle of the roof. How hard it was to build the church of 1709—1772, and how rude it was when built, is obvious from the fact that the first tax of a penny in a pound was spent in procuring the nails. Another vote respected the glass and lead. Another directs that " it be ceiled with good sawn boards on the within side up to the railings and filled with mortar up to the girts." Later thoughtfulness of our fierce northwesters suggested the vote that the mortar should be continued along the second story. Two tiers of new seats were ordered, one on each side the aisle which extended to the east door. It follows from this and other notices, that the house stood along the street to the northwest of this, that the pulpit was on the west side and the entrances were from the north and south and east.* In 1731 the purchase of a bell was ordered, and in 1738 a town clock. Before the bell was provided, the beat of drum called the people together on Sundays and public days at a cost of £1 10s. the year. New seats are next ordered for the gallery : now and then a pew is erected at the expense of the occupants.† In 1746 a commit-

* The seats from the first house were probably removed to the second and were placed facing the pulpit, except the two new ones, which, it may be conjectured, filled the space not covered by the old seats, now transferred to a larger house. Mrs. Whitman, the pastor's wife, sat in a pew at the south, i. e., the right hand of the pulpit, but this pew was built at Mr. Whitman's expense, and after his decease it was purchased by the society.

† In 1759 the society ordered all the seats except those in front to be pulled down and replaced by pews.

tee was appointed to repair the house and see what can be
done " to prevent its spreading." From that time onward it
was doomed to destruction. It was neither large enough nor
good enough for the community which was beginning to be
conscious of wealth and strength and which was rapidly grow-
ing in its resources and its ambition. It was time that the
old structure of unpainted boards on its sides within, and its
naked rafters or joists above, should give place to something
better.

At the time when this church was built, the original town
of Farmington was as yet undivided, extending from Simsbury
on the north to Wallingford on the south ; from Wethersfield
and Middletown on the east to Harwinton and Waterbury on
the west, about fifteen miles square. Within this township
were the parishes or parts of parishes of Kensington, New
Britain, Southington, New Cambridge, Burlington, and Northington. The town meetings were held in this village, which
was as large or larger than it is at present, and felt a motherly
pride in, and perhaps asserted somewhat of a motherly authority over its full-grown daughters, who were now settled in
their separate homes. The wealth of the town was considerable
though neither trade nor manufactures had made any special
progress, there being in the village only two or three merchants. The Grand Lists for the years 1778–1780 indicate
no overgrown estates but many thriving households. The new
settlements in Litchfield county from 1720 onward must themselves have opened valuable markets for the products of this
fertile valley and these smiling slopes.

The as yet imperfect roads and the few not very comfort-
able vehicles, rendered communication with Hartford, Wethersfield, and New Haven somewhat difficult, and shut up the
town to the development of its own resources and the cherish-
ing of its own independence. It was a fit thing that this
large and flourishing parish of this large and flourishing town
should erect this capacious and stately meeting house as the
expression of its public spirit and its well developed resources,
to say nothing of the nobler motives which beat strongly in
the heart of the staunchly puritan community,—reverence for

the dreaded Jehovah and faith in his fidelity to those who honored his day and his ordinances. The parish was large and every " Sabbath-day" hundreds came from every quarter to fill this spacious house. From Red Stone Hill and the Great Plains on the southwest, from Lovelytown on the far north-west-through the Langdon Quarter, from Scott's Swamp to the line of Bristol, from the woods of Burlington on the west, from the remotest Eastern Farms, from Cider brook on the river, from the distant parts of White Oak to its mountain pass and along its mountain slope, and from all the many farm houses and thrifty farms between—more numerous and more thrifty than now, with families that also were far more numerous then, trooped every pleasant Sunday morning hundreds upon hundreds, the elders on horseback, with their wives on pillions behind, the sturdy sons on half-broken colts and the daughters on the gentler fillies, now and then a household in a heavy farm wagon laden with half a score—till seven or eight hundred filled up the pews below and swarmed in the galleries. The Sabbath was the gathering day for the tribe, for to the duty of waiting on the Lord Jehovah all were drawn by social excitement, as well as prompted by conscience and duty, by habit and tradition, by the fear of God and of man. Whosoever in the large parish failed to be an habitual attendant at this one house of prayer showed most unmistakably that he feared not God neither regarded man. He became literally a social outlaw. His house and his farm were regarded as accursed, for he had deliberately disowned the covenant and forsaken the temple of the living God!

Soon after the War of the Revolution, with the returning activities of peace, this town became the seat of an extensive trade. The town which had guarded the frontier undauntedly for three-fourths of a century in face of an Indian village and the dark forest of the Mohawks beyond, now began to command the trade of the new towns that were springing up in every part of that forest. From along the Litchfield turnpike on the west—the turnpike which, as long as New York and its vicinity was held by the English, was the high road from Boston and Hartford to the Middle States—down the valley of

the Tunxis from the northwest towards Pittsfield and Albany,
up the Farmington from the north and across the Great Plains
from the south and southeast, there was gathered an active
mercantile trade which was first set in motion by John and
Chauncey Deming, who were followed by the five sons of
Elijah Cowles,* and the two sons of Solomon Cowles.† Some
of these merchants set up branch houses in the neighboring
towns. Some, not content with buying their goods at Hartford and New York, arranged to import them and in their
own vessels. The signs on the numerous stores bore the in-
scriptions of " West India and East India goods," and in some
instances these goods came directly to the hands of the Farmington merchants. At one time three West India vessels at
least were owned in Farmington, which were dispatched from
Wethersfield or New Haven. One at least was sent to China,
and brought from the then far distant Cathay, silks and teas,
and Chinaware bearing the initials of these daring importers.
The Indian corn which was raised so abundantly in the
meadows and on the uplands was extensively kiln-dried and
sent to the West Indies, and with the horses and the staves
which the then new near " West " could so abundantly furnish,
was the chief export which brought back sugar, molasses, and
Santa Cruz rum. At a somewhat later period an active trade
in tinware and dry goods, was pushed into the Atlantic Southern States and employed the energies and excited the ambition of many of the young men of the village and the town.
Large fortunes were occasionally the results of these ventures.
Not infrequently the young man who went forth in the ma-
turity of strength and the confidence of hope, never returned!

The old meeting house began to rustle with silks and to be
gay with ribbons. The lawyers wore silk and velvet breeches;
broadcloth took the place of homespun for coat and overcoat,
and corduroy displaced leather for breeches and pantaloons.‡

* Seth, Elijah, Jonathan, Gad, and Martin.

† Solomon and Zenas.

‡ Breeches of deer and calf skin were very common a century since as we learn
from the faithful testimony of Governor Treadwell respecting the dress of that
generation (1802). (See Porter's *Historical Discourse*, pp. 81, 82, 83.) We
gather from the old account books, that the price of making a pair of leather
breeches was about 4 shillings, and of a dressed deerskin, was 20 shillings.

As the next century opened, pianos were heard in the best houses, thundering out the " Battle of Prague" as a *tour de force*, and the gayest of gigs and the most pretentious of phaetons rolled through the village. Houses were built with dancing halls for evening gayety, and the most liberal hospitality, recommended by the best of cookery, was dispensed at sumptuous dinners and suppers.*

The military spirit of the town was fostered by its wealth and enterprise. Upon this meeting-house green on the first Mondays of May and September, and some one or two other days in the autumn, there were gathered the three military companies of the town—the Grenadiers, select and self-respecting, glorying in the buff and blue of the Revolution, with a helmet of more recent device but of Roman model—the Infantry, or bushwhackers, numerous, miscellaneous, and frolicsome, whose straggling line and undisciplined and undisciplinable platoons were the derision of the boys and the shame of all military men—and a small but select company of cavalry, or " troopers," as they were called in contrast with the " trainers." These last consisted of " the horse taming" young men of the community—more commonly sons of farmers in the remoter districts, who delighted in the opportunity to show their horsemanship, and thus vie with the aristocratic grenadiers

---

* This period of active business and mercantile enterprise and the rapid accumulation of wealth extended from 1790 till about 1825. In 1802 Governor Treadwell records that "a greater capital is employed in [trade] than in any inland town in the State." Mr. Chauncey Deming was first among these merchants for strength and positiveness of character and for business ability. He was foremost in enterprise, and was an active and influential director in one of the banks of Hartford and Middletown. During the War of 1812, all the banks of the State except the Hartford Bank suspended payments in specie, and it is confidently asserted that Mr. Deming held large specie reserves in Farmington, which he produced from time to time to save the credit of the bank. No one who ever saw him in his vigorous old age as he galloped along the street upon his strong and elegant horse, or as he sat in church, with his powdered queue and his bright blue coat with gilt buttons, will forget the impression.

The decline of this trade began with the opening of a more ready communication with Hartford, by the extension of the Litchfield and the Albany turnpike roads over the Talcott Mountain. The Farmington capitalists were large owners in the stock of both these roads. They did not foresee that by making it easier for themselves to go to Hartford, they would make it easier for their customers to do the same.

who were more largely from the village. In the autumn also was the annual " field day " for the regiment. which was summoned to meet once a year on one of the immense rye fallows that stretched out upon the Great Plains.* To these military organizations the meeting-house was in some sense the center. The minister was summoned yearly to offer prayer upon the Green amid the assembled three companies and invited to dine with the officers and those aspiring privates who chose to indulge in the expense of a dinner for a trifling sum. Should it rain on training day beyond endurance the meeting-house was opened to protect the soldiers from a drenching. These walls have many a time reverberated to drum and fife and the tramp of files along the aisles, while excited boys looked down from the gallery with wonder at so strange a spectacle, breathless with misgiving at the disturbance of their wonted associations with the place.

Around the meeting-house were gathered representatives of all the population on the three or four days of Election week in the Spring, and the two days after the annual Thanksgiving in the autumn. The Election days were usually devoted to ball-playing, in which adults participated with the zest of boys, and delighted to show that their youthful energy was not extinct, and that the tales of their youthful achievements were not mythical exaggerations. Wrestling matches, throwing of quoits, and other feats, were by-plays to the principal performances. Even the holidays and sports of the village were under the shadow of the meeting-house and sanctioned by its vicinity.†

Recollections and associations like these attach themselves

---

* The consummation of the military glory of the village was reached when it could boast of a Major General whose staff was largely made up from its wealthy young men. The distinguished white horse on which the General rode contributed not a little to the glory of the General and his staff. However sober and prosaic this horse might seem during most of the months of several of his last years, he never failed to grow young and gay as the autumnal reviews required his services.

† We are obliged to add that the punch and toddy which were freely distributed on these occasions were often "brewed " on the steps and at the doors of the sanctuary. But we are glad to be able to say that among the hundreds who assembled on such occasions it was rare to see any one intoxicated.

to every village church and village green in Christendom. These are uniformly the central gathering places for the community that dwells around them. But the Puritan meeting-house of a New England village, it should be remembered, held other relations to the community than those of a place of worship. These special relations we may not overlook in commemorating one of the few of these old Puritan meeting-houses which was erected at a time when these influences were fully recognized, and in which they have continued as long as in most of the New England towns. The Puritan meeting-house was freely used for other assemblies than those convened for religious worship, for the reason that the Puritan believed so fervently in the application of Christian principles to all the departments of life. These truths were, first and foremost, to be applied to the inner springs of action in the heart; next, to the external conduct; and last, but not least, to the ordering of that self-governed society of freemen, the New England town, which, in the heart of the Puritan, was honored as an ordinance of God.

When the Puritan community built its meeting house, it devoted it primarily to the uses of religious worship—primarily but not exclusively, for if it could also serve the political or the educational necessities of the community better than any other edifice, it was freely employed for such uses. To close the doors of the sanctuary against assemblies of this kind was regarded by the Puritans as gross superstition, akin to the idolatry of the altar and the priesthood.* The New Eng-

---

* It may abate the horror of a certain class of readers to learn that the custom of holding parliamentary elections in the parish churches was even recently by no means uncommon even in England. I quote from a well known author: "The poll was to be held in the church—a not uncommon usage in country boroughs —but which, from its rarity, struck great awe into the Kingswell folk. The church warden was placed in the clerk's desk to receive votes."—*Memoir of John Halifax, Gentleman,* chap. xxiv. A town meeting in the times of the American Revolution is thus described by John Trumbull :

> High o'er the rout, on pulpit stairs,
> Mid den of thieves in house of prayers,
> *   *   *   *   *   *   *
> Stood forth the constable ; and bore
> His staff, like Mercury's wand of yore.
> *   *   *   *   *   *   *
> Above and near the Hermetic staff

land town meeting. which was sagaciously recognized by De Tocqueville as the germ from which was developed our American political life, was uniformly held in the meeting house. This was not merely nor mainly because the Puritans in the early days had no other place in which to assemble, but because the work which was transacted there had the most intimate relations to the kingdom of God, and because it was transacted with the gravest dignity and in a religious spirit. The town meeting was uniformly opened by prayer and occasionally made memorable by a sermon. The first sermon which was printed by the Rev. Dr. Porter, was delivered in this house in 1815. Its subject was ' The Sin of Perjury, in violating the Freeman's Oath.'

The Puritan did not honor the house of Christian worship as such by superstitious reverence. He was careful not to uncover his head in the week time when he entered its walls, for the same reason that he would not bow to what was called an altar because he deemed it a sin to worship any material semblance or symbol. But if he did not reverence the house as a structure, he was careful to honor it when it was used as a place of worship. When the Lord was in His holy temple, he never forgot that he should keep silence before Him. No man was more careful in his attendance or more reverent in his demeanor when God was present with His people in His house, or when Christ had come into the midst of two or three disciples who were assembled in His name.

It is singular that those who are most ready to charge the Puritans with unchristian irreverence for their free use of the meeting-house are also most forward to charge them with Judaical superstition. In principle they were less Judaical than their opponents. Both were Judaical in a degree, but the non-ritualistic Puritans least of the two. The opponents of the Puritans treated the church as a temple, the eucharist

> The moderator's upper half
> In grandeur o'er the cushion bowed
> Like Sol half seen behind a cloud.
> Beneath stood voters of all colors,
> Whigs, Tories, orators, and brawlers.
> *McFingal*, Canto I.

as a sacrifice, its administrators as priests qualified to mediate between God and man by virtue of an apostolic succession, and holding the keys of the kingdom of heaven through sacramental rites. The Puritans protested that the hour had already come when men should no longer say that in Jerusalem only men ought to worship, and that all men worship the Father who worship Him in spirit and in truth. Concerning the state, their opponents held that it was ordained of God in the Jewish way, by hereditary descent and divine right,—symbolized by priestly anointing. The Puritans held that as in the church, so in the state, it was from the free election of its constituent members that all its rulers proceed, and to the the decisions of its organized assemblies alone divine authority belong. That the iconoclastic zeal and the zealous protests of the Puritan may not have led him to excess in the disregard of consecrated places and of outward observances, I do not contend ; but that, as between the two, the non-conformist was the least of a Jew and a devotee of superstition, we may fairly conclude. While both parties were Judaical in their spirit, the Anglican was a Jewish ritualist, who clung to forms and rites with minute punctiliousness; while the Puritan was a Jewish prophet who boldly and sternly rebuked everything which might take the place of spiritual worship, and searched the heart with the severest scrutiny. Neither had effectually learned that the Christian church has not " received the spirit of bondage unto fear, but the spirit of adoption," which is also a spirit " of power, of love and of a sound mind."

But whether we approve or condemn, the fact cannot be questioned that the regular town meetings were held in this edifice till 1830, when the society politely bowed out the town by placing at its disposal the Union Hall in the Academy building. It is worthy of notice, however, that at the first meeting of the parish after the dedication, in December, 1772, it was voted to give the town the materials from the old church for building a Town House on this plat. It is probable that the parish was more moved in this act by its concern for the newly finished edifice, than by any feeling of its special sacredness. There was soon pressing and frequent occasion

for town meetings that were anxious and thronged ; meetings
that were grave and solemn,—in which the help of God was
required and fervently sought for. Scarcely had this house
been dedicated by this community when, after a brief respite
of some ten years from the sacrifices and exposures of wasting
war, it was excited by those more alarming premonitions
which, in two and a half years, were followed by the contests
at Lexington and Bunker Hill. These contests were preceded
and followed by a succession of town meetings in which this
house was thronged by excited multitudes, and this green
was dotted by earnest groups and crowds, now whispering
and pointing to this and that suspected traitor, or gesticu-
lating with determined resolve. Among the resolutions that
were debated and passed the following are significant :

"At a very full meeting of the Inhabitants of the Town of Farmington, Legally
warned and held in said Farmington, the 15th day of June, 1774, Colonel John
Strong, Moderator :

Voted, That the act of Parliament for blocking up the Port of Boston is an In-
vasion of the Rights and Privileges of every American, and as such we are Determined to oppose the same, with all other such arbitrary and tyrannical acts in
every suitable Way and Manner, that may be adopted in General Congress : to
the Intent we may be instrumental in Securing and Transmitting our Rights
and Privileges Inviolate, to the Latest Posterity.

That the fate of American freedom Greatly Depends upon the Conduct of the
Inhabitants of the Town of Boston in the Present Alarming Crisis of Public affairs : We therefore entreat them by Every thing that is Dear and Sacred, to
Persevere with Unremitted Vigilence and Resolution, till their Labour shall be
crowned with the desired Success.

That as many of the inhabitants of the town of Boston, must, in a short
time be reduced to the Utmost Distress, in Consequence of their Port Bill, we
deem it our indispensable Duty, by every Effectual and Proper Method, to assist
in affording them speedy Relief.

In pursuance of which Fisher Gay, Selah Hart, Stephen Hotchkiss, Esqs., and
Messrs. Samuel Smith, Noadiah Hooker, Amos Wadsworth, Simeon Strong,
James Percival, Elijah Hooker, Mathew Cole, Jonathan Root, Josiah Cowles,
Daniel Lankton, Jonathan Andrews, Jonathan Woodruff, Aaron Day, Timo-
thy Clark, Josiah Lewis, Hezekiah Gridley, Jr., Asa Upson, Amos Barnes
Stephen Barnes, Jr., Ichabod Norton, Joseph Miller, William Woodford, Jedidiah
Norton, Jr., Gad Stanley, John Lankton, Elnathan Smith, Thos. Upson, Elisha
Booth, Samuel North, Jr., Theo. Hart, and Resen Gridley, be a committee, with
all convenient speed, to take in subscriptions : Wheat, Rye, Indian corn, and
other provisions of the Inhabitants of this Town, and to Collect and Transport
the same to the Town of Boston, there to be delivered to the Select Men of the

Town of Boston, to be by them Distributed at their Discretion, to those who are incapacitated to procure a necessary subsistence in consequence of the late oppressive Measures of Administration.

That Wm. Judd, Fisher Gay, Selah Hart, and Stephen Hotchkiss, Esqs., Messrs. John Treadwell, Asahel Wadsworth, Jonathan Root, Sam. Smith, Ichabod Norton, Noadiah Hooker, and Gad Stanley, be, and they are hereby appointed a Committee to keep up a Correspondence with the Towns of this and the neighboring Colonies, and that they forthwith transmit a copy of the votes of this Meeting to the Committee of Correspondence for the Town of Boston, and also cause the same to be made public.

Sept. 20, Tuesday, 1774, it was voted that the Selectmen be directed to purchase Thirty Hundred weight of Lead to be added to the Town stock for the use of the Town.

At the same meeting, voted, that the Selectmen be directed to procure Ten Thousand French flints to be added to the Town Stock for the use of the Town.

Voted, That the Selectmen be Directed to purchase thirty six barrels of Powder, with what is already provided, to be added to the Town Stock for the use of the Town.

On the 12th day of December, 1774, this town by their vote did approve and adopt the doings of the Continental Congress, held at Philadelphia on the 5th day of September last; also, on the same day, it was voted

Whereas, upon a vote of the Town of Farmington assembled in Town Meeting on the 12th day of December, 1774, to adopt the doing of the Continental Congress, one Matthias Loaming, and Nehemiah Royce, utterly Refused to vote for the same, we do therefore Consider them as Open Enemies to their country and as such, we will, according to the Resolution of the Congress, from this Day forward, withdraw all connection from them, untill they shall make Public Retraction of their Principles and Sentiments in the matters aforesaid.

On the 26th day of December it was voted, that the town would leave it to the inspecting committee to determine every matter and thing respecting Torys during the town's pleasure.

At a meeting of the inhabitants of the town of Farmington, held March 26th, 1777. At the Same meeting, the Rev. Sam. Newell and Timothy Pitkin, Messrs. John Trendwell, Noah Porter, Hezekiah Wadsworth, Jonathan Root, Jehiel Cowles, Timothy Clark, Noah Cowles, Oliver Hart, Elijah Hooker, Asa Upson, Amos Barnes, Ichabod Norton, Tim. Thompson, Jacob Foot, Joseph Woodford, Col. Lee, Maj. Stanley, Stephen Barnes, Jr., Simeon Hart, and Moses Deming, be a committee to take into consideration the regulations of his Honor the Governor, and Council of Safety, dated March 13th, 1777, and to report their opinion, etc.

This meeting was by vote adjourned for one hour and a half, and met according to adjournment. Upon the report of Said Committee, it was voted that the Sum of ten pounds lawful money be given by this town to every able-bodied, effective man inhabitant or residing in this town, in addition to the several encouragements already given, that shall voluntarily enlist in the Continental service in the 8th battallion, for three years, or during the present war, so far as shall be necessary to supply our quota of 217 men; and also the like sum of ten pounds of lawful money to be given to all who have already enlisted within this town that are recorded toward such quota, provided a number of men sufficient to supply the deficiency of our quota as aforesaid can by such encouragement be obtained; to be raised by a tax on the sales and rateable estate of the inhabitants of said town, and to be collected as soon as may be; and when collected, to be deposited in the treasury of s'id town, to be under the direction of a committee appointed for that purpose, five pounds of which bounty to be paid by said committee to such persons respectively as shall hereafter enlist themselves as aforesaid, on their enlistment if collected, and the other five pounds to be paid to such persons at the end of one year after their enlistment, and when the quota is completed as aforesaid, the like proportion of such bounty to be paid to them that have already enlisted.

At the same meeting, voted, A tax or rate of four pence and a quarter on the pound on the last list, to be collected and improved agreeable to the above vote.

And at the same meeting, voted, a rate of four pence and one farthing on the pound on the same list agreeable to the above vote.

At the same meeting, voted, that Messrs. John Treadwell, Noah Porter, and Solomon Whitman, be, and they are hereby appointed, a committee to draw on the treasury of this town in favor of such soldiers as have or shall enlist into the Continental battallions for three years, or during the present war, agreeable to and in pursuance of, the votes of this town this day passed.

At the same meeting, voted, That Samuel Smith, Martin Bull, Capt. Treadwell, Noah Cowles, Elijah Hooker, Jonathan Root, John Curtiss, Asahel Barnes, Stephen Hotchkiss, Esq., Capt. Wm. Woodford, Timothy Thompson, Elnathan Smith, John Richards, Simeon Hart, John Ward, Stephen Barnes, Jr., Jacob Foot, and Thomas Upson, be a committee to take care of the several families of the soldiers that have or may enlist into the Continental army, when they shall be properly applied to, and see that they are supplied with necessaries at the price stated for by law, without any additional cost, and that all the additional cost be paid by the town.

At the same meeting, voted, that all such persons as shall enlist into the Continental service to fill up the 8th battallion, be freed from paying any part of the tax or taxes granted by this meeting.

At the same meeting the following resolve was passed and voted, viz:

Resolved, That we do mutually pledge our faith and honor to each other and to our country, that we will ourselves conscientiously observe and obey the laws of this State for preventing oppression, and will use every measure that is proper and effectual in our power, to see that the violators of said laws be brought to condign punishment.

On the 22d of Sept., 1777, it was voted, that the committee be directed to provide two shirts and two pairs of stockings for each soldier belonging to the Continental army that are enlisted for three years or during the war.

Also, voted, that the said committee be empowered to procure the articles mentioned in the said regulation, without being limited to any price.

At the same meeting Capt. James Stoddard and Samuel Curtiss were, by vote, chosen constables for the present year.

In 1775 special encouragement was given to John Treadwell and Martin Bull, in the manufacture of Saltpetre.

Sept. 16, 1777, the first record is made of the administration of the Oath of Fidelity to the state of Connecticut, and the oath provided for freemen to a large number of persons.

A similar record is made Dec. 1st, 1777, and others at subsequent dates.

The inhabitants of the town of Farmington in legal town meeting convened. To Isaac Lee, Jr., and John Treadwell, Esqs., Representatives for said town in the General Assembly of this state. Gentlemen having in pursuance of the recommendation of the Governor of this State taken into serious consideration the articles of confederation and perpetual union proposed by the Honorable Congress of the United States to the consideration and approbation of said States, we are of the opinion that there is much wisdom conspicuous in many of said articles which in many respects are highly calculated to promote the welfare and emolument of the United States and promise the most extensive blessings to us and posterity, it is therefore with the utmost pain that we find there is discoverable in some of said articles which bear an unfavorable aspect to the New England States, and this in particular, the similarity of customs, manners and sentiments of the nine Western states, and their opposition to the New England States in these respects, especially as the power of transacting the most important business is vested in nine states, gives us great apprehension that evil consequences may flow to the prejudice of the New England States—the method of appointing courts for the deciding controversies between two or more states which will, as the case may be, entirely exclude every person that may be nominated in the New England States; the rule of stating the quota of men for the Continental Service in war and mode of apportioning of the public expense, we are constrained to say are in our opinion very exceptionable though we are unwilling to believe that they were designed for the prejudice of this and the other New England States; you are therefore directed to use your influence in the General Assembly of this State by proper ways and means that the articles of confederation may be amended and altered in the several particulars above mentioned by Congress, if such emendations can be made without manifestly endangering the independence and liberties of the United States. The emoluments, however, of the United States are to govern you in all your deliberations upon this interesting and important subject.

Voted, That the other articles of confederation are approved with the exceptions above taken in these instructions.

April, 1778.   Test. Sol. Whitman,
                                                        Town Clerk.

A meeting of the inhabitants of the town was held on the 30th of August, 1770, to take into consideration the unhappy circumstances of the British Colonies, etc., etc., and in particular the request of the Committee of Merchants desiring a meeting of the mercantile and landed interests of the several towns in this colony to be convened at New Haven on the 13th of September.

Mr. Jonathan Root and Fisher Gay were chosen, and a long series of very spirited resolutions were passed, some of which were directed against the purchase of goods supposed to be imported in violation of the spirit of their agreement, and the encouragement of hawkers and peddlers who might introduce such goods without license.

That these resolutions called forth much earnest discussion, and that the walls of this house resounded with exciting appeals and noble demonstrations we cannot doubt. Fore-

most among those who acted and spoke was the Colonel Gay
who had been so conspicuous in the construction of this
edifice. At the first summons from the east he raised a company at once, repaired to the scene, and afterwards became
Colonel of a regiment of the Continental Army under Washington. As the army was transferred to New York he stopped
a night or two at home, and though indisposed, would not be
moved by the appeals of his family to remain, but rejoined
his regiment and soon died in the hospital near New York.
That he was ardently patriotic and public-spirited, self-sacrificing and gallant, was attested by all who knew him. Alike
ardent in counsel and foremost in every good work in this
community, whether it concerned the School, the Church, or
the State, he cheerfully risked his life for the rights of New
England and the independence of the United Colonies. Nor was
he alone. Three companies from Farmington were in action
against Burgoyne, and it is confidently asserted by one whose
recollections cannot be mistaken, that every young man from
the town, worth any consideration, was at some time or other
in the field. That some of these companies and detachments
of men were assembled in this house before they were sent
forth, and that all were paraded upon this green and commended to God in prayer, is certain. The fluent and eloquently
fervid pastor of this church, Mr. Pitkin, was sent for to Simsbury to preach the farewell sermon to the soldiers of a company, raised just after the battle of Bunker Hill. Concerning this gathering we have the words of an eye witness : " At
the hour appointed, we marched to the meeting house, where
the officers appeared in military style, with their appropriate
badges of distinction, and the soldiers in proper order, with
their arms and accoutrements, as men prepared for battle. It
was a full and overflowing audience, and all in high expecta-
tion of hearing something new and charming from so gifted a
preacher. After his warm and fervent prayer to heaven for
the success and prosperity of the American armies, and the
liberties and freedom of our country, he introduced his address,
if I remember right, from these words : ' Play the man for
your country, and for the cities of your God; and the Lord
do that which seemeth him good.'

This sermon was well adapted to the occasion and spirit of
the day. It was tender and pathetic—lively and animating.
It was like martial music; while it touched the finer feelings,
it roused and animated for the dreadful onset—the shout of
war and the cry of victory! During the time of its delivery,
abundance of tears were seen to flow, from both old and
young, male as well as female."*

That similar scenes were transacted within and without
this house none of us can doubt. who have been so recently
witnesses to their like in our recent conflict. Earnest prayer
was offered on every Lord's day for the fathers and sons who
were in the field, and at the interval between the services
the latest news from all the places of contest was eagerly com-
municated and heard. This village street was a part of the
high road from Boston through Hartford to Philadelphia.
Washington came by this route to meet Rochambeau at Wethersfield to arrange for the final expedition against Yorktown.
Several thousand of the French troops were encamped for a
night at least, about a mile below this place, and their arrangements for a bivouac are still to be seen. Tradition says that
the Puritan misses did not disdain a dance by moonlight with
the French officers. Some of Burgoyne's officers were quar-
tered here after the surrender, and we are indebted to the skill
of one of their number for two of our best houses. Several
dwellings were patterned in different parts of the State after
one of these houses. A part of the artillery taken at that
memorable surrender was kept for a long time in the village, in what was formerly the orchard of John Mix.

Farmington was a staunch Federalist town till the Federalist party was set aside. Two or three of the leading men
only were Jeffersonians, but they had a slender following.
That this was largely owing to the influences which issued
from this old meeting house, would certainly have been con-
ceded, or rather angrily contended by the anti-Federalists.
Whatever religious advantages might have followed the
division of the parish into two or three religious denomina-

---

* See Barber's Historical Collections of Connecticut, (Simsbury).

tions. it is morally certain that had any other house of worship been erected here, the town would have been divided into two political parties. As it was, John Mix, the town clerk, who wrote a bold clerkly hand, and Gen. George Cowles were regularly sent to the Legislature for more than a score of years. Hon. Timothy Pitkin was for several sessions a Federalist member of the United States Congress, and after his retirement from political life was of no doubtful political sympathies. His always lighted candle, as it gleamed from his office every night, testified to the passers-by of laborious historcal and political researches, all of which were made to contributed to the renown of the party of Washington and Hamilton.

To the Puritan meeting house the school house was always an indispensable adjunct and a near neighbor. Upon every village green the school house was built under the shadow of the house of God. The holy commonwealth of the Puritan could not discharge its duty to itself and its Redeeming King did it not provide by law and taxation for the instruction of the children of all its households. The Puritan town and the Puritan parish, as soon as either attained to organized life, provided for the instruction of the children as well as for the maintenance of worship, and enlisted the active co-operation of minister and magistrate. This old meeting house has witnessed a special and also an historic interest in this class of duties. Within six months after its dedication the parish was divided into separate school districts, and a petition was presented to the legislature to authorize each to tax itself to manage its own concerns. It was not till 1795 that the Legislature constituted special school societies throughout the state. In the year following, this newly formed school society digested a system of regulations for the visitation and discipline of the schools. In 1798 a bill with similar provisions was reported by John Treadwell of this town, afterwards Governor, and adopted for the entire state of Connecticut. This edifice deserves especial honor as the place in which the school system of Connecticut was first matured and adopted.

The town of Farmington provided very early and very liberally for a special town fund for the support of public schools

5

in all its societies, by the sale of lands reserved for highways. In this old meeting house also were held the annual school exhibitions, in which the highest classes from all the schools, each in turn, appeared on the stage to try its skill in reading, spelling and defining before the assembled community. The late Professor Olmsted records his remembrance of one of these exhibitions which must have taken place before 1809.* The one which I remember must have been held before 1817. It was fixed in my memory by the circumstance that the first class from the school on the Plains could not be accommodated on the narrow stage that was stretched in front of the pulpit from gallery to gallery, but a large number stood in the aisles below at each end. In February, 1793, it was voted that John Treadwell, John Mix, Timothy Pitkin, Jr., and Seth Lee be a committee to devise a plan for the formation of a new school in the society to give instruction in some of the higher branches of science not usually taught in common schools and report. There is no record that any report was ever made. It is probable that the fierce ecclesiastical strife which had begun to agitate the community, preoccupied the attention of the public.†

In the year 1816 the academy building was erected by an association of gentlemen who contributed a thousand dollars, to which the society added some six or seven hundred ; thereby securing to itself the use of a convenient lecture room and to the community apartments for a higher school. Such a school was maintained with great success for some twenty years, and was of great service to this and other towns. To this movement may be directly traced all that has been subsequently done for special education in this village.

Of this academy the most distinguished principal was Deacon Simeon Hart, who not only devoted himself with singular painstaking and probity to the education of the youth committed to his care, but was in all his years of residence in this town a public-spirited citizen, and an ardent servant of

* See Half Century Discourse, by Noah Porter. Appendix, p. 45.

† See page 51.

Christ and his church. No man loved this old meeting-house better than he, or delighted in whatever might contribute to the spirituality and attractiveness of its worship, or the success of the gospel. His pride in the historic memories of this edifice and this town prompted to very laborious services in preserving these memories from neglect and oblivion.

The relations between the meeting-house and the academy were so intimate that when it became desirable to accommodate the large audiences which were attracted by the annual public exhibitions, the meeting-house was opened, and dramas were more than once enacted in this old Puritan edifice with drop curtains and green room. Many hundreds of pupils from places near and remote have habitually worshiped in this sanctuary and have learned to remember it most vividly. Not a few have been attracted by its teachings and worship, to a higher and better life on earth and in that kingdom which Christ has opened to all believers.

The Old Red College, as it was called, should not be forgotten, as its inmates at one time made themselves very conspicuous in this meeting-house and in the community. It stood on the ground now occupied by the Female Seminary, and was originally the residence of Col. Noadiah Hooker. His pure and noble-minded son Edward Hooker used it for lodgings for a number of students from the Southern and South-Western States, whom for several years he prepared for college and for public or professional life.

In the palmy days of the village these well-dressed and showy young men, ten to fifteen in number, for several years made themselves conspicuous at all times and especially on Sundays, when with iron-shod boot-heels they tramped to the highest pew in the gallery and made themselves the observed of all observers.

The meeting-house certainly befriended the public libraries which this village has for a long time most successfully sustained. One of these for a long time satisfied the literary wants of the North end of the village, but was subsequently absorbed into what was called the Phœnix Library, which has existed since early in the present century. I think there was also a Mechanics Library in the village, and still another library on the Great Plain. One of these libraries, probably the oldest, originated in a horse-shed with a few boys, as I am informed, who organized a plan of joint ownership and exchange for the very few juvenile books which came within their reach. It became a very flourishing institution, and was for many years sustained by a large number of proprietors. They met for many years on the first Sunday evening of every month at the house of Deacon Elijah Porter.* This library meeting was the village Lyceum at which its educated and professional men and the more intelligent citizens would freely compare their views in respect to the affairs of the village and the nation, to which thoughtful and curious boys listened with unnoticed attention. After this free interchange of opinion, which went on while the books were received which had been taken at the previous meeting, at the appointed hour the drawing began, which was now and then interrupted by an active bidding for any book which was especially desired.

The old library still survives in the hands of a very few of the original proprietors. It is an instructive memorial of the past as well as a valuable collection of standard books.† It is to be hoped that it may never be dispersed but may become the property of the town. It would not be honorable to the town or the village at a time when so many towns in New England are collecting and supporting public libraries if these books

---

* On the records of the Farmington Library Company, there appears on page 1, a "Catalogue of the Library begun in 1785." On the 1st of January, 1801, without any apparent change in the organization, it began to be called the Monthly Library. From 1796 to 1813 Elijah Porter was the librarian. During the year 1813 the office was filled by Luther Seymour, after which the library was dissolved, and on the 12th of February, 1814, the Phœnix Library was formed by a selection of the more valuable books from the old library. Elijah Porter was again appointed librarian and retained the office until March 17, 1826, when the Village Library, of which Capt. Selah Porter had been librarian since January, 1817, was united with the Phœnix and both remained under the care of Capt. Porter until he resigned April 4th, 1835, and Simeon Hart, Jr., was appointed in his place. It appears by the record that "The Farmington Library Company was formed Feb. 18, 1839, designed to supersede the Phœnix Library Company, which proved defective in its organization and was accordingly dissolved."

† See the Report of the Secretary of the State Board of Education, A. D. 1868, page 94.

should be sold for a pittance, and its standard histories and solid treatises should be distributed no one knows whither. At the time when it was most generally used there were no daily newspapers in Connecticut. No religious newspapers were in existence. A monthly magazine brought scanty news of the movements of the Kingdom of Christ. The mail came from Hartford and all the world besides but once a week in a coach drawn by two horses.*

The meeting-house also educated the people through the Westminster Catechism, which was recited every Saturday morning in all the public schools—due allowance being made to the few who preferred another manual. Once in the winter the minister regularly catechised all the schools as the Pastor of the lambs of the flock, and inspected them in his capacity as school-visitor. From 1810 to 1818 special catechetical exercises were maintained by the church for all the baptized children.

In 1818 a Sunday school was established, and has ever since been prosecuted with great vigor and eminent success. Subsequently Sunday school libraries were introduced, and afterwards Sunday school newspapers and numerous other appliances, till the Sunday school has practically become one of the regular services of the Lord's Day.

The meeting-house contributed to the education of the people most efficiently by its direct instrumentalities, by the Sabbath neatness, and order and decorum which it enforced, by the universal respite from secular occupations, and by the well-reasoned sermons which were pronounced from the pulpit to

---

* It was not till the year 1823 or 4 that a line of four horse stage coaches was established from New Haven to Northampton, which ran through the town three times a week each direction, and afterward every day. Another similar line to Litchfield also was established about the same time. The former was a forerunner of the Farmington Canal which was commenced in 1825, completed to the State Line in 1828, and subsequently finished to Northampton in 1834. In 1848 this canal was abandoned and the Canal Railroad was completed to Plainville, to Collinsville in 1849, and to Northampton in 1858. The relations of the canal to the old meeting-house ought not to be entirely overlooked. In the earlier years of its existence it did good service by bringing to church, in a boat, made convenient for the purpose, a large freight of passengers from Plainville who beguiled the voyage by singing and other religious services.

hundreds of thoughtful listeners. The arguments of these sermons concerned the immortal interests of men—their appeals waked up the most stirring emotions. Many of their hearers during the following week pondered on what they heard, and esteemed the words of the preacher more than their necessary food. For more than one generation while this edifice has stood, the Sunday sermons took the place which is now largely usurped by books, and newspapers and social intercourse. The truths which were discussed in this pulpit, the principles which were enforced, the quickening seed-thoughts which were uttered, the kindling and elevating pictures which were portrayed, and the eloquent expostulations which were sent home to the heart, furnished of themselves an education the value and efficiency of which cannot easily be over-estimated. If theology is the haven and Sabbath of all man's contemplations, then a theology earnestly and plainly preached is of itself an efficient instrument of culture.*

The New England pulpit has usually been an instructive pulpit. The New England ministry has not usually failed in definite opinions, or feared to utter them. The New England meeting-house has been the sanctuary of the freest and boldest discussion of all the truths which bear upon man's salvation in the life to come, or his duties in the life that now is. The boldness and independence of this ministry have been its strength. It has neither sought to soften the truth nor to conceal it, but by manifestation of the truth has commended itself to every man's conscience in the sight of God.

This leads me to notice what this old meeting-house has

---

* It is not easy for the present generation to conceive it possible that the interest in theology should be so absorbing among many of the leading men of a community as we know it was till a comparatively recent period in many of the New England parishes. Certainly it was so during two-thirds or three-fourths of the century while this meeting-house has been standing.

The rigidly orthodox Governor Treadwell could not receive without an elaborate metaphysical protest the new-light notions of the distinguished theologian of the parish of New Britain, but held an earnest controversy with him in the Connecticut Evangelical Magazine. One of the early remembrances of my life is of a visit to the Pastor from Deacon Bull who had been endeavoring to digest the newly-published, and as he thought, the new-fangled theology of Dr. Dwight, in a borrowed volume which he brought home with his queries and exceptions.

contributed and what it has witnessed in the way of forming and reforming the public morals. If the Puritan minister was at times over definite and confident in laying down the doctrines of the gospel in all the ramifications of a metaphysical system, he certainly did not shrink from expressing his mind in regard to the duties which the gospel enforced, nor in applying its rules to the lives of his own flock. There certainly has been no deficiency in this meeting-house in this regard. If the merchants and capitalists of Farmington were ever lax in inserting certain descriptions of property in their tax lists, it was not for the lack of faithful admonition from the Pastor. If the youth were tempted to excessive laxity in amusements they heard a timely word.*

When the attention of the churches of New England was called to the ravages of intemperance, this church responded with zeal to the summons. When the first and second and third temperance movements were made, viz :—abstinence from distilled liquors, from everything which can intoxicate, and the Washingtonian reform ; this meeting-house heard many a sermon from the pastor on the Sabbath, and many an address, and a discussion from the pastor and others on week days in respect to the teachings of the scriptures and the legitimate deductions from them. This meeting-house was efficient in driving out the numerous distilleries which once filled the parish and the town, as well as in making the indiscriminate sale of liquors to be disreputable. Whatever any man may think of some extremes in principle and temper which may have been exhibited in this movement, no one can doubt that the movement itself has done much to redeem the community from a blighting curse.

* On the days of the Annual Fast the political sins of the commonwealth and of the nation, especially after both had fallen off to Jeffersonian principles, were duly set forth in many pulpits ; not very offensively in this. One Congregational minister in Connecticut—the eccentric but shrewd Dr. Backus—the minister in Bethlehem, subsequently President of Hamilton College, was betrayed into such bold utterances concerning President Jefferson, as to be prosecuted for libel and committed by the United States marshal to the jail at Hartford for the lack of the bail which he refused. Being somewhat eccentric in his humor and being provided with a swifter horse than his guardian, he amused himself on his way from Litchfield to Hartford in occasionally leaving the marshal a few miles behind.

The Anti-Masonic movement agitated the community somewhat painfully, although the glories of the Farmington Masonic Lodge had begun to decline when the excitement against masonry commenced. The meeting-house and the church witnessed somewhat earnestly against this association, although a few years before, the meeting-house was filled with a crowd at a magnificent celebration of St. John's Day by a masonic procession which took possession of its seats and its pulpit, and symbols mysterious to the boys were paraded before uninitiated eyes and the Rev. Menzies Rayner delivered a discourse from Gen. XIII., 8.

The Anti-Slavery movement was taken up at an early period and prosecuted with great earnestness.* This and Anti-Masonry occasioned decided differences of opinion in respect to the interpretation of the Scriptures and the proper attitude which should be assumed by the church toward masonry and slave holding. These differences were attended by many uncomfortable results and not a little excited feeling. Whatever any one might then think, or may now think of the utterances of the pastor in respect to either movement, no one could doubt that he endeavored to find the truth with an honest and earnest love of the truth, and that when he formed an opinion he did not hesitate to utter it with boldness on the one hand, and on the other with a liberal and charitable love for those who were not content with his moderation. In these reforming efforts the old meeting-house has heard some utterances from the pulpit and the pews which had been more wisely suppressed. But the free spirit of the fathers taught their sons to prove all things, and hold fast that which is good. Those of the hearers whose patience has been tried and whose spirits have been stirred by the too much, or the too little which has been set forth in the name of God, have generally

---

* It deserves to be remembered also in the annals of this house that after these agitations had begun to subside, some forty Africans who had been set free by the authority of the nation, were regularly present in it for months, as an earnest of the great deliverance which was to follow a quarter of a century afterward. When these Africans became residents of this town, and every Lord's Day appeared in this house of Christian worship, their presence was felt to hallow this place, and gave emphasis to the oft repeated prayer, " Thy Kingdom come."

bethought themselves that a free pulpit, and a bold pulpit bring more of good than of evil to a community, and that some of the most important lessons which the gospel teaches are those of tolerance and charity when party feeling runs high and good men are tempted to suspect and denounce one another. The old meeting-house has outlived so many passing excitements even in this unexcitable community as to be able if it would, to emblazon on each panel of its extended walls some wholesome lesson concerning the folly of hotheaded wrath in the name of Christ, and the sublime wisdom of quietly resting in the truth that is or may be revealed. The sum of the gathered wisdom of its century of observation upon these discussions and differences of opinion in regard to Christian and political ethics is the apostolic direction. " Let us therefore as many as be perfect be thus minded, and if in anything ye be otherwise minded God shall reveal even this unto you."

One class of difficult duties this pulpit has faithfully inculcated, for the exercise of which this meeting-house has been a successful school of practice. I speak of the duties of Christian benevolence at home and in foreign countries. It is not easy to conceive what were the conceptions and habits of this community sixty years ago in respect to this class of duties. But we must do this in order to appreciate what changes this meeting-house has witnessed. At that time the community was more wealthy than it is at present, but the yearly salary of its minister was five hundred dollars in money, the use of the parsonage, and twenty-five cords of wood ; the whole being the equivalent of say twelve hundred dollars at the present time. Once a year by authority of the Governor of the state, a contribution was called for in behalf of the Domestic Missionary Society of Connecticut. There existed also a Female Cent Society somewhat later to which each subscriber paid a cent a week or fifty cents a year. At the anniversary of this association each contributor sent or paid in her subscription, enclosed in a paper parcel with her name written within. The contribution of now and then a dollar would betoken some special elevation

6

of the grace of liberality in the heart of some devout mother in Israel.

The American Board for Foreign Missions and the Connecticut Missionary Society for the new settlements gleaned up scanty collections, and the Connecticut Bible Society paid its occasional members in illegible Bibles at a reduced price.

It was not an easy thing in times like those for the pastor of such a congregation as this to stand up before the assembled hundreds whom he had known from boyhood and urge the duty of greater benevolence, and to do this persistently in the name of his master, who though he was rich, yet for our sakes became poor. But he did it perseveringly amid cold, incredulous, and scowling looks, and the reward of his fidelity was great. The old meeting-house has been, in an eminent sense, the treasury house of the Lord, and many who have waxed liberal under its influences have been greatly enriched of the Master. This meeting-house has also trained the people to good manners. The youth stood up before their elders. Mr. Pitkin, while he continued the pastor and long afterward, walked with dignity up the center aisle in flowing cloak and venerable wig, with his three-cornered hat in hand, bowing to the people on either side.

This meeting house has also enforced respect for age and position by the traditional custom of *seating the people*.

On finishing the old meeting house, that is, the second, the society appointed four men as a Seating Committee who were "to do it by their best discretion." A year after when the report came in, it was voted that the society "do regret what was done by the last Committee in seating of the meeting house," also that the new committee "shall have respect to age, office and estate, so far as it tendeth to make a man respectable and to everything else which hath the same tendency." The committee were requested "not to divulge their report until it is made public to the society, when the society shall accept or reject it."

This rule of seating was re-enacted in 1783–4, and occasionally afterward. In 17ᴢ3, February, a large committee was appointed to *dignify the meeting house*, that is, to designate and arrange the seats according to their relations of dignity, and to report. Their report was received at a subsequent meeting and a seating committee was immediately appointed; so difficult was it to adjust this difficult matter. The society persevered in thus seating the church as long as it defrayed its current expenses by taxation. The last seating took place in 1842. In December, 1844, the society voted to rent the pews. In 1805 Lieut. Gov. Treadwell with his lady was invited to sit in the minister's pew during the pleasure of the society, and there he sat till his death. In 1821 Solomon Langdon, the distinguished benefactor of the society, was invited to take his seat in the same pew. The seating of the meeting-house according to age and position was a significant practice in the olden time, for by it that respect to the aged and the honorable, which is inwardly felt in every community not wholly barbarous or wholly rotten, was formally and outwardly expressed by a place in the meeting-house, and sanctioned every Lord's Day in the presence of God. Those times were at least stable when society was held together by bonds like these, for though occasional envy and disparagement might be cherished in secret they could not overthrow an arrangement which commended itself to the judgment of the solid men of the community and was conformed to the traditions of their childhood. When the minister or stranger entered the school house, its busy inmates rose at once to their feet. As either approached the school house by the way-side the school children ceased from their sports and arranged themselves in ranks to give a pleasant greeting to the passer-by— a greeting which blessed those who gave more than those who received it. These customs of deference and honor, of courtesy and respect, did much to soften the rugged aspects of Puritan life. They lifted up its stern and uncompromising democracy into the dignity of an organized society. They restrained the unblushing impudence of untamed boyhood and disciplined all classes to respect for the laws and to obedience to God. The family, the school, the meeting-house, society itself were nurseries of order and decorum. We cannot revive these decorous customs if we would. We would not if we could, but we cannot but greet them as they pass in review before our memory with the words :

> " Hail ancient manners ! Sure defence
> When they survive of wholesome laws."

There are some who do not share this feeling, but would ridicule the pedantic stiffness and tenacious aristocracies of Puritan society. Others would denounce them most emphatically as unchristian and unseemly in the house of God. But the fashionable church of modern times with its guarded pew has little to boast of improvement in its new way of *seating the meeting-house,* flaunting as it does the wealth which often *does not make a man respectable* by ticketing on his pew the price which he pays for his sittings.

There was one grievous exception to the general decorum which was enforced by the old meeting-house, and that was the behavior of the youth and children in the galleries. It was one of the inconsistencies of the Puritan's theory with his practice, that in theory he included the children and youth within the blessings of the covenant with the family and the church, and in practice cast them out of the family circle in the house of God at the most critical and exposed period of their lives. This practice is akin to its singular straining of the evidences of the beginning of the Christian life which practically prevented so many from taking upon them the vows of the Christian profession till a later period, and led many to do this even then in a superficial way, who should have been encouraged to appropriate all the blessings promised to the believer. The old gallery of the Puritan meeting-house has too often been little better than a veritable *Court of the Gentiles* into which the children were banished, there to be systematically trained by the arrangements for their accommodation to regard themselves as mere lookers on in the sanctuary. The gallery was the perpetual cross to the young minister and the old ; to the grave elders below, and to the perplexed tithing man who could ill conceal the vexation, to betray which would but weaken his authority.* It is not easy

---

* These occasional outbreaks among the youth in the galleries are in part to be ascribed to the rude and vigorous life and the exuberance of animal spirits which

to explain the introduction of this practice of separating the
youth from their families and sending them into this outlying
wilderness. In the older countries, both in Germany and
England, the galleries are largely the preferred seats. Distinguished personages very frequently have their pews aloft.
But the first Puritan meeting-houses were rude and inconven-
ient, and the Puritan's knowledge of architecture did not
enable him to make the galleries accessible or attractive.
The aged, who were pre-eminently the honorable with the
Puritan, would naturally not desire to ascend a difficult stair-
way. We find within the historic period that the gallery of the
Puritan meeting-house was usually filled with the least reverent
hearers and was oftentimes a place of open trifling. In this
town so early as 1714 the deacons were requested " to appoint
or persuade some persons who by the seating shall sit convenient to inspect the youth in the meeting-house on days of public worship and endeavor to keep them in order." Again in
1716-7 the society made choice of Thomas North, son of Samuel, to inspect and keep the youth in order in the lower part
of the meeting-house, and Samuel Orvis and Simeon Newel
for the same service in the galleries. In December, 1772, the
first month after this edifice was occupied it was voted that
the center pew in the front gallery shall belong to the men,
and the following stern resolve was adopted, " whereas it is
suggested by many members of this society that indecencies
are practiced by the young people upon the Sabbath in time
of public worship by frequently passing and repassing by one

belonged to the hardy sons and daughters of other generations. Beneath all the
decorum and stiffness which were imposed by artificial manners and religious austerity there was no little rudeness in the outbreaks of youth when they fell short
of criminal excess. An earnest defender and yet a discerning critic of Puritan
life says very acutely, " When our fathers tried to make the youth of a whole
community as grave as church members and moreover by law, it was a similar
mistake. Hence we find the reaction, the outbreaking of violent pleasure the
more sure as the more forbidden. I have heard old men tell amidst the coercive
austerity of the day of wash-tubs set on chimnies, frogs dropped on ashes, cart
wheels taken off, walls built across public roads, and all the freaks of rustic mis-
chief, the *flash and outbreak of a fiery mind* in youth, when age is, or is thought
to be, too severe." *The Puritan: By John Oldbuy, Esq.* [Rev. Leonard Worth-
ington, D. D.] No. 23, Boston, 1836.

another in the galleries, and intermingling sexes to the great disturbance of many serious and well minded people—Resolved and Voted, that each and every of us that are heads of families will use our utmost endeavor to suppress the aforesaid evils and will strictly enjoin it upon all persons under our care to behave decently on the Sabbath or Lord's Day, and that the different sexes for time to come neglect to pass up and down the gallery stairs other than those that lead to that part of the gallery assigned for different sexes, as they will avoid the displeasure of this society, and be accounted disturbers of the peace of said society and liable to be proceeded against as such." In 1813 it was voted " that the practice of certain young gentlemen in seating themselves in the pews on the female side of the gallery in times of public worship is disorderly, and ought to be, and is, by this society, wholly disapproved of." In 1824, the matter of the galleries was taken thoroughly in hand and a committee was appointed for the purpose " of securing better accommodations and better order in the house of God." As a consequence, important alterations and extensive repairs were made. The remote pews against the walls, which in some churches have often been no better than the devil's playhouses and hiding-places, were removed. Families were henceforth seated in the galleries; room was thus made for the youth with their parents above and below. Special seats were also assigned to those who were older. In consequence, order and decorum were thereafter effectually secured. This was a most important improvement which doubtless grew out of the great change in the religious feelings of the community which occurred in 1821, and signified that new relations had been established between the children and youth of the congregation, and the pastor and elder members. That so great an innovation should have been introduced at so early a period in this large community is most honorable to the enterprise of the pastor and the energy and moral force of the congregation.

Much attention has been given to sacred music especially since this meeting-house has stood. At times the singing has been of marked and acknowledged excellence. Many of the leading men in the community delighted in music, and were no mean proficients in directing it. I have heard from a gentleman who was well informed on the subject that the choirs of Farmington and Wethersfield were greatly distinguished and maintained an active rivalry at times for preeminence.

But the singing at public worship has not always ministered to the harmony of the congregation. Here, as elsewhere, the efforts to effect a concord of sweet sounds have resulted in fierce discord between sensitive tempers. Music has been the subject of frequent discussion, and has been a fruitful occasion for temporary troubles. In March, 1726–7, was passed the following minute: "This meeting taking into consideration the unhappy controversy that hath been among us respecting singing of Psalms in our public assemblies upon the Sabbath, and forasmuch as the church in this place hath several times in their meetings manifested their dislike of singing psalms according to the method not long since endeavored to be introduced among us being the same way of singing of psalms which is recommended by the reverend ministers of Boston, with other ministers to the number in all of twenty or thereabouts ; therefore that the controversy may be ended, and peace gained for this society, this meeting by their major vote do declare their full satisfaction with the former way of singing of psalms in this society and do earnestly desire to continue therein, and do with the church manifest their dislike of singing according to the said method endeavored to be introduced aforesaid."* In 1757,

*How unhappy these controversies were will be apparent from the following : "To the Honourable yᵉ General Assembly at hartford yᵉ 18th of May 1725. the memorial of Joseph Hawley one of yʳ house of Representatives humbly sheweth your Memorialist his father and Grandfather & yᵉ whole Church & people of farmingtown have used to worship God by singing psalms to his praise In yᵗ mode called yᵉ Old way. however t'other Day Jonathan Smith & one Stanly Got a book & pretended to sing more regularly & so made Great disturbance In yᵉ worship of God for yᵉ people could not follow yʳ mode of singing. at Length t'was moved to yᵉ church whither to admit yᵉ new way or no, who agreed to suspend it at least for a year. yet Deacon hart yᵉ Chorister one Sabbath day In setting yᵉ psalm attempted to sing Bella tune—and yoʳ memorialist being used to yᵉ old way as aforesd did not know *bellum* tune from *pax* tune, and supposed yᵉ deacon

the society voted and agreed that they would introduce Mr.
Watts' Version of the Psalms to be sung on the Sabbath and
other solemn meetings in the room of the version that hath
been used in time past. At the same meeting Elijah Cowles
was requested to tune the Psalm, and that he shall sit in the
fifth pew. In 1762 Mr. Fisher Gay was chosen to assist
Elijah Cowles in setting the psalm, and he should sit in the
ninth pew on the north side the alley, and Stephen Dorchester
was chosen to assist the choristers in reading the psalm. In
April, 1773, the spring after this house was first occupied a
choir was allowed by the following vote. "Voted that the

had aimed at Cambridge short tune, and set it wrong, whereupon yᵉ petitioner
Raised his Voice in yᵉ sᵈ short tune & yᵉ people followed him, except yᵉ sᵈ Smith
& Stanly, & yᵉ few who Sang allow'd In bella tune ; & so there was an unhappy
Discord in yᵉ Singing, as there has often bin since yᵉ new singers set up, and yᵉ
Blame was all Imputed to yoʳ poor petition [er] , and Jnᵒ Hooker, Esqʳ assistant,
sent for him, & fined him yᵉ 19th of febʳʸ Last for breach of Sabbath, and so yoʳ
poor petitionʳ is Layed under a very heavie Scandal & Reproᵃch & Rendered vile
& prophane for what he did in yᵉ fear of God, & in yᵉ mode he had bin well educated in and was then yᵉ setled manner of Singing by yᵉ agreemᵗ of yᵉ Church.

Now yoʳ Petitionʳ thinks yᵉ Judgement is erroneous, first, because yᵉ fact if as
wicked as mʳ hooker supposed Comes under yᵉ head of disturbing God's worship,
& not yᵉ statute of prophaning yᵉ Sabbath : secondly, because no member of a
Lawfull Church Society can be punished for worshiping God In yᵉ modes &
forms, agreed upon, & fixed by yᵉ Society. thirdly because tis errors, when yᵉ
Civill authority sodenly Interpose between partyes yᵗ differ about modes of worship, & force one party to Submitt to y other, till all milder methods have bin
used to Convince mens' Consciences. fourthly because tis error to make a Gent
of yoʳ petitionʳ Carractᵉr a Scandalous offender upon Record, for nothing but a
present mistake at most, when no morral evil is Intended.

Wherefore yoʳ poor petitioner prayes you to set aside yᵉ sᵈ Jud, or by what
means yoʳ honʳˢ please, to save yoʳ poor petitionʳ from yᵉ Imputation of yᵉ hein-
ous Crime Laid to him, & yoʳ poor petitionʳ as In duty &c. shall ever pray.
JOSEPH HAWLY

This Assembly Grants the Prayer of the within Petition.
Past in the Lower House.
Test,   THO. KEMBERLY, Clerk

Re-considered. Dissented to in the Uppʳ House.
Test,   HEZ. WYLLYS, Sectʳʸ

Capt. Timiᵗ Pierce, Messrs. Whittlesey & D. Buell, are appointed a Comᵗᵗᵉᵉ
from the Lower House to confer with such Gent as the Upper house shall appoint
upon the differences of the houses on the above Petition, and make report to
this assembly.
Test,   THO. KEMBERLY, Clerk

people who have learned the rule of singing, have liberty to
sit near together in the same position as they sat this day at
their singing meeting and they have liberty to assist in carrying on that part of divine worship." What this "position"
was will occur at once to those "old inhabitants" who remember
the long line of singers around the front of the gallery which
was marshaled and controlled by the chorister opposite the
pulpit, assisted by a few leading singers. At times this line
would be greatly abbreviated and demoralized. Again after
a fresh impulse given by " a singing school," its well-filled
ranks would stretch all along the front, composed of "young
men and maidens, old men and children."

Mr. Martin Bull was appointed to lead, and John Treadwell
and Asahel Wadsworth to assist as there should be occasion.
But alas! very soon, in December, 1774, a large committee was
required to compromise " the difference among the singers."
At the same time it was voted to sing at the close of the
second service in the winter as well as in the summer. In
1793 six dollars were appropriated to purchase several copies
of Barlow's Version of the Psalms of David, and distribute
them among the singers, having regard to the most deserving.
In 1795 the society's committee are directed to have an accomplished master to instruct in psalmody. In 1803 eight choristers were appointed, Luther Seymour at the head. In 1811
a large permanent committee was appointed to regulate the
singing in every particular. In 1818 the Handel Society
was organized, under the leadership of the eminent Dr. Eli
Todd, and was invited by the society to conduct the service
of song, which it did with great acceptance.* Dr. Todd did
not sing himself but led the choir by his violin, the use of
which was then a novelty in a Puritan meeting house.

* This society was very numerous, and the members occupied all the seats in
front of the pulpit; Dr. Todd having drawn the long and straggling line into a
compact mass in the center of which he stood, animating and swaying all by his
eye and his instrument. Dr. Todd was reported to be an infidel at that time and
had rarely attended church although he was the beloved and trusted friend of the
pastor. It was a matter of great rejoicing in this sensitive community when he
pledged himself to conduct the singing, and the zeal for the Handel Society was
in part inspired by the interest felt in this eminent and greatly beloved physician.

The violoncello was introduced about this time with the flute, the clarionet and bassoon. In 1822 the Handel Society gave notice that it would no longer sustain the singing, when four choristers were appointed, Horace Cowles at the head. In 1825 liberty was given to the choir to choose its own leader during the pleasure of the society. In this way came into being what was known as the Associated Choir, the existence of which is manifest on the records of the society in 1841. This society received liberal appropriations for several years, but some differences having arisen which could not be adjusted, its services as an association were dispensed with by vote of the society in 1846. Unhappy controversies having followed this event, the society in 1851 passed some conciliatory resolutions expressive of their high estimate of the value of the service of this body, inviting its members to unite with the existing choir. In 1852 resolutions of a more positive and earnest character for conciliation and adjustment indicate a serious disturbance of feeling among the singers in the society. In 1861 an organ was purchased, by voluntary subscription from the ladies and an appropriation from the society.

But excitements about singing, or other subjects, have not been able to weaken the stability, or disturb the unity of this parish. The old meeting-house is a fitting symbol of the generally enduring compactness of this ecclesiastical society. For a century it has stood unmoved against the blast of many a fierce northwester, neither shaken from without, nor rent within. In how many bright moonlight nights has it steadied itself against the threatened wrath of the invading foe. How often has it been shaken in its every timber by the rushing winds, when fair weather has come out of the north with terrible majesty. Often have the spirits of the air made infernal music in its mazy attic, and howled in fiendish merriment over its impending fall; but it has not fallen. So has the parish stood amid all the heavings and rockings from without and within. Its stability and peace have been usually the envy of its neighbors, and an example to all lookers-on. There are meeting-houses in Connecticut which have been little better than houses of contention and wrath; in which

Christ has literally been preached of strife and vain-glory, and the hearers have literally experienced to the full the warning, "but if ye bite and devour one another, take heed lest ye be consumed one of another." There are so-called houses of worship which one shudders to look at or think of, so completely have they been made the devil's houses for bitterness and party feeling, instead of being the dwellings of Christian peace and love—churches which one or two bad men, or one or two wrong-headed or stiff-headed good men have continued to keep in a turmoil which has made its Sunday worship a feast of bitterness, its preaching a series of personal denunciations, and its prayers ebullitions of wrath against man, rather than offerings of love and humility before God. The good sense and Christian feeling which have ruled in this community have delivered this meeting-house from such shocking desecration, and have secured to the parish the steady fruits of temperate wisdom. Above all the spirit of God has been present more than once by timely interposition to bring peace to this house. Not long after this house was erected, after the close of the Revolutionary struggle, the parish was rent by a protracted strife with and about Rev. Allen Olcott, who was the minister from 1787 to 1791.* Four years afterward the divisions were still more threatening, for they were aggravated by a sharp and positive hostility on the part of many influential men against the new light or Hopkinsian preaching. Mr. Edward Dorr Griffin, afterward so distinguished and so well known, preached as a candidate in the fervor of his youth, with the glow of his soaring imagination, and the brilliancy of his imposing rhetoric. His preaching was attractive and powerful ; and it made a strong impression on the young and the old. Many were awakened to new convictions and began, as they thought, a new life. Many were vexed and disturbed and conceived a determined hostility to the fearless and defiant preacher. The old strifes were re-awakened and became more bitter than ever. A decided majority gave Mr. Griffin a call; but a large minority opposed him —73 to 24. He accepted the call after a delay of nearly five

* See Porter's Historical Discourse, pp. 78-9.

months. A council was convened which declined to install
him against so strong an opposition, but advised the calling of
another council, to which the society consented by a small
majority—the vote standing 62 to 41. Meanwhile some re-
ports were circulated unfavorable to the character of Mr.
Griffin, and his opponents made use of them before the council. When this body convened, the house was packed as never
before or since with an excited auditory. The spokesman for
his opponents was arrayed in full professional attire and made
showy denunciations against Mr. Griffin's reputation. The
council acquitted the candidate of the charges, but advised
that he should withdraw his letter of acceptance, which he
did, and the storm was allayed. In a few months after, in the
same year, Rev. Joseph Washburn came among this people a
messenger of peace and of blessing—a man of quiet dignity
and winning ways—who united all hearts, exorcised the spirit
of bitterness and dissension, and brought peace to the parish.
Soon after the present century opened, while unity and strength
reigned within there were many fears from without. The old
standing order which was supposed to be the necessary support of the original parishes of the state was actively assailed.
Many fears were cherished that if the new party should pre-
vail the churches would be invaded or torn down. One of
the leading Hartford newspapers in the interest of the Federal
party frightened its confiding readers with a picture of the
Toleration party just come to power and proceeding to tear
down the churches and burn the bibles. The people of this
parish were mostly Federalists; but in case they should be
released from the obligation to support some church by taxation, none could foresee how many would refuse to be taxed.
This release was secured in 1818 by the constitution of the
state which was adopted that year. Previous to this event,
while the storm was preparing from afar, Mr. Solomon Langdon had given the society property to the value of $2,500, of
which the income alone was to be used. In 1820, after the
new constitution had been adopted, he offered $500 more on
condition that a fund amounting to $10,000 should be raised
and properly invested. The conditions were complied with.

Subscriptions were made by all classes and almost every individual. Subsequently the fund was increased by $2,000 more. It was supposed when this was accomplished that the gospel was provided for forever in this parish, and the joy that was felt and expressed showed how earnestly the hearts of this great parish were interested for the future of this community. The necessity of increased expenditures has prevented this fund from being so great an evil as it might have been. The zeal with which it was raised in what was supposed to be a critical period is worthy of all honor. The agitations and fears and divisions which have occasionally sprung up have been chiefly uncomfortable because of the good which they hindered than because they have seriously threatened the permanence or the unity of the parish.

But the religious life of the community is that which the meeting-house is designed to promote. The spiritual worship offered from one Lord's Day to another, the renewal of better aspirations, the renunciation of besetting sins and inveterate habits of evil, the strengthening of the faith, the brightening of the hopes, the maturing of the patience, the re-kindling of zeal, the training of the believer for a better life on earth and a more precious inheritance in heaven—these constitute the true glory of the house of prayer. We ask then with special interest what has the old meeting-house achieved and what has it seen, of results of this kind during the century in which it has resounded with public prayer and praise. The answers to these questions have been given so fully in the published discourse* of the pastor who served you sixty years, that I need only refer to what you know so well. Some fifteen or sixteen hundred have been added to the communion of the church. The largest number at any one time was 114 in 1821 on a bright Sabbath in June. Of these there were representatives from almost every house of those who had been moved to the before untried exercises of prayer and praise in

* See Memorial of a Revival—A Sermon by Noah Porter, pastor of the Church in Farmington. Hartford, 1822: also Half Century Discourse; on occasion of the fiftieth anniversary of his ordination as Pastor of the First Church in Farmington, Conn. Delivered November 12th, 1856, by Noah Porter, D. D. Hartford, 1857.

that wonderful revival of religion which came into this community as a rushing mighty wind and caused its population to speak with new tongues of the wonderful works of God. Then was eminently fulfilled, " the Lord whom ye seek shall suddenly come to his temple, even the messenger of the covenant whom ye delight in." Before and since, this house has often been hallowed with the presence of the Holy Spirit. Many men in their sturdy strength have learned to sit at the feet of Christ with docile spirits. Many old men have waked to new views of life. Many, very many children and youth have been gently led into the ways of blessed Christian aspiration. Here truth has been patiently explained and earnestly commended to hundreds who have found it confirmed in their own experience and much of it has sprung up and borne abundant fruit. There are many thousands scattered here and there over this broad land, and some in other lands who have been made better men and women and whose households are better and happier for the impressions received or confirmed in this house. There are multitudes of perfected spirits now gathered to their rest above, who can remember seasons spent in this house which were the anticipated earnest of that which they now enjoy in the great assembly of the Redeemer. Surely God has been in the place though we have not known it. Christ has often been here and the Holy Spirit has brooded over and within this house by his life-giving power.

During all this century the Christian church has been learning new lessons of Christian truth and of the Christian life. It is no dishonor to the worthies of the past to believe this. It would be a fatal defect in the gospel and would argue that it was not from God were it not progressive. The traditions of our fathers and the spirit of our Congregational polity enjoin upon us the duty of opening our minds and shaping our actions to every new revelation which is made concerning the word of God and the life of truth and obedience. This meeting-house has seen great changes in the speculative and practical views of Christendom, and it has not only accepted many of these changes for the better, but it has rejoiced in them as relieving Christian truth from many objections, and the Christian life and character from unfortunate misconceptions and reasonable reproach. Your old pastor in his Half Century Discourse confessed to have made important changes in his theoretical and practical views during his long ministerial life, and recorded his unfeigned regret at many of the imperfect and one-sided exhibitions which he had given of the gospel in the earlier part of his ministry.* He rejoiced that he had entered into more satisfying and rational views of Christ and his salvation. But no man doubted that with each advance which he made, he made progress in spiritual knowledge and in Christian simplicity; that he became more humble, more Christ-like, and more self-sacrificing the longer he lived; that he was stronger and more clear in his faith and love, even though he was more playful, more humane, and more catholic till the last day when he ministered from this pulpit. The old meeting-house has been true to the duty of forgetting many things that are behind and reaching after those that are before. It has witnessed and has contributed to a progress of opinion in respect to Christian theology and Christian living which would deserve thanks and congratulation this day did we but walk in the brighter and better light which has been gradually breaking upon the Christian church since the foundations of this edifice were laid.

It has been a distinguished honor to this old meeting-house that it has so long been the sole place of Christian worship for an undivided parish. It has been a peculiar privilege of its ministers to be regarded as the pastors of all the souls within this community. While so many of the old New England parishes were divided and sub-divided into diverse denominations; when so often out of every local or neighborhood quarrel

* Very instructive impressions of the practical views entertained of the nature and process of conversion and of the cardinal doctrines of the Gospel when this meeting-house was first erected may be obtained by reading the account of the revival of religion in Farmington, in the year 1799, prepared by Rev. Joseph Washburn, and published in the Connecticut Evangelical Magazine, Vol. 1, pp. 378, 420. A very careful and sagacious estimate of the doctrinal and practical views which were generally accepted in the New England churches before this period, covering the first twenty-five years after 1772, is presented in a paper by Rev. Luther Hart. Quarterly Christian Spectator, 1833, Vol. 5, No. 2, Art. 3.

there would follow a sudden conversion of a score of families to some new views of Christian doctrine or ordinances or polity; when the shepherd of the flock was so often worried out of his life by the well-meant but ill-judged arts of prose-lyting on the part of some three or four rival competitors for the patronage or the caprice of unstable souls; when three or four houses of worship have so often drained the resources, and divided the sympathies, and awakened the jealousies of a scanty population; when every visitation of the divine spirit was certain to be followed by an unholy scrambling for new accessions to this or that Christian communion; when in almost every parish of New England was repeated the scan-dal and the shame of Protestant Christendom in its petty division into manifold sects; it was for nearly three-fourths of a century the glory of this meeting-house that within its ample inclosure all the people were gathered for worship and rejoiced in the same shepherd and pastor. Even when a few families constituted another religious society, this sense of unity was scarcely disturbed. The members of the old parish contributed nearly as freely to the erection of the new meeting-house as though it had been a chapel of their own and its existence has never awakened any feelings of jealousy or strife. The time is fast approaching when these unseemly divisions among those who hold one faith and one Lord, must give way before the pressure of a common foe from without or be consumed under the re-kindled and awakening zeal of the new life from within; when the assumption by the several sects to exclusive claims will be signally rebuked by the mas-ter, or abandoned before the sharp judgments of his provi-dence; when the duty of mutual compromise and united action and fellowship will bring together many of these half-starved churches, and put an end to their warfare on one another and indirectly upon the cause which they profess to serve.

Much also might be said in view of the history of this old meeting-house, of the workings of the self-governed church which was the mother church of New England. Were we to take the history of this parish and this church for two hund-

dred and thirty years and review it in the spirit of impartial
criticism, we might safely challenge Christendom to produce
any better results under any other polity or from any other
organization. We would not forget the excesses which have
come from over-heated zeal, or party strife, or disturbing and
ambitious leaders, or covetous worldliness, or unchristian hostility to the truth. We would make the largest concessions
to what might be urged against the austere spirit and narrow
systems of the fathers, and against the lax libertinism, and
the worldly compliance of their sons. We would concede
that there has been something of priestly denunciation and of
lay intermeddling, and that strife and division have occasionally wrought their evil work. But we may still look with
pride upon the honor which the history of the church brings
upon the polity and principles which it has tested for a century
past. The men whom it has trained in its school of thought
and action—the women whose saintly piety and efficient benevolence it has cherished and inspired—the families whom it
has blessed by its simple worship and its friendly care—the
poor at home whom it has fed and comforted—the feeble
churches at a distance which from the first it has fostered and
befriended—the unenlightened to whom it has sent its living
messengers and its never-failing contributions—the oppressed
whom it has remembered in their bonds—the country to which
it has been true in the years of its peril—the hundreds of men
and women who in every part of the country are ready to
rise up and bless it—these are witnesses to what one of these
New England churches has accomplished. We glory in our
" mother church " for similar works which she has done in
hundreds of communities. We are not blind to its defects,
nor would we propagate it as a sect to the destruction or weak-
ening of a single Christian household. We care for it most
of all because it is so unsectarian in its spirit and large-hearted
in its charity, and because by its simple organization it so
readily adapts its views of Chrisian truth, its modes of worship
and its conceptions of Christian culture and of Christian duty
to whatever Christ is continually teaching his church by his
providence and spirit. We believe that something like it will

8

be eminently the church of the future—when the living and present Christ shall come nearer to his people and they shall live more consciously in his presence and for his kingdom. Perhaps this old church which has so sturdily withstood all physical decay for a hundred years may not need to survive another century to witness a united Christendom—when in every village there shall be but one fold and one shepherd; when all shall be re-baptized with the spirit of the Master and fulfil His prayer for his disciples " that they all may be one, as Thou Father art in me and I in Thee, that they also may be one in us. that the world may believe that Thou hast sent me."

During the existence of this meeting-house the parish has more than once been peacefully divided. New churches have been constituted which regard this church in a very special sense as their mother. There are a few among the members of each of these parishes who never pass this meeting-house without a blessing, or think of the old gatherings on Sunday without a leap of the heart, as they recall the times when the long trains of wagons brought in their hundreds of worshipers and carried them home with pleasant remembrances of social fellowship and of Christian incitement. There are many from the parishes which still belonged to the old town of Farmington when this church was raised and whose fathers gathered here to take the Oath of Fidelity to the state of Connecticut, headed by their ministers, and joined in the same committees for the service of the country, and went to the field at a moment's warning. Few of the descendants of these families have forgotten the traditions and associations which connect them with this church and this meeting-house. The thrift and sagacity which have brought such large accessions of wealth and of population to these neighboring communities—the Christian zeal and liberality for which they are distinguished—the love of order and education and the best features of the old New England life which they have cherished, are all in no small degree to be ascribed to the influences which have proceeded from this meeting-house green, and very largely from this meeting-house. No inhabitant of

the old town who knows anything of its history or cares anything for the New England traditions can fail to hail the old
church as it completes the past century of its life. There are
others still—emigrants from this once flourishing community,
and the children of emigrants, and their children's children,
who themselves or their ancestors have worshiped in this
house, but in the earlier days settled in Vermont, or a little
later spread themselves along the great avenue that was opening westward through the Empire state, or have been scattered through what were the forests of Ohio, Michigan, and
Indiana, or distributed along the prairies of the Great Valley, or impelled to the Pacific shore, to whom this old meeting-house is cherished with sacred associations, whether it is
a blessed memory or an image hallowed by the loyal affection
of honored kindred.

We may not conclude without a more distinct reference to
the deceased pastors of the church who have done so much
to make this meeting-house a blessing to the community.
When the house was dedicated, the courtly and fervent Mr.
Pitkin had been pastor of the church for twenty years. His
fluent and animated exhortations and his earnest piety were
esteemed and honored in it thirteen years afterwards.* When
the Revolutionary war was over, he was dismissed at his own
request, but he continued to reside in the village; sat in the
pulpit and rendered occasional acceptable services to the
church till he died in 1812, forty years after the church edifice was finished. Then followed ten years of party strife
and low morals and worldly prosperity† till the ordination of
Mr. Washburn, whose winning manners and saintly elevation
brought many accessions to the church, and a great and lasting blessing to the community. After ten years he died and
for a generation was mourned by many and is yet not alto-
gether forgotten by a few.‡ In 1806 Rev. Dr. Porter was
ordained the pastor. The vote by which he was invited to
accept the office was thus phrased: "Voted that this society,

---

* See the sketch of his life in Porter's Historical Discourse, p. 77.

† The same, p. 78.

‡ See Porter's Historical Discourse, p. 79.

from personal acquaintance with Mr. Noah Porter, Jr., *being one of us,* and from sufficient experience of his ministerial gifts and qualifications, are satisfied that he is eminently qualified for the work of the Gospel ministry, and do now call and invite him to settle with and take the charge of the people of this society in that important work." And in this spirit he was received and supported till his death. I need not refer to any further particulars of the events of his ministry for the first fifty years, for he has recorded them fully in the sermon which was preached at the expiration of that period. I need not describe his character; he was known and read of all men, and there were few who did not honor and love him. That he loved this church and delighted in this meeting-house you need not be told. It was providentially ordered that the afternoon appointed for his burial was so inclement that his remains, which had been brought to this house for the public religious services, were detained till the following morning before they were consigned to the earth. A few of the parishioners and friends kept watch during the night. It was fitting of itself that these remains should rest awhile in this place where for more than eighty years he had been an habitual worshiper, and for sixty had served as pastor. It is confidently believed by some

"That millions of spiritual creatures walk the earth
Both when we wake and when we sleep;
* * * * * * * * *
* * * * * * and oft in bands
While they keep watch, or nightly sounding walk,
With heavenly touch of instrumental sound
In full harmonic numbers join their songs,
Divide the night and lift our thoughts to heaven.

If this is true, surely on that night there were gathered in this house the spirits of other generations to renew with their pastor the worship in which he and they had united when present here in the body. With him they reviewed all the memories of the past, and recalled the scenes which had hallowed these walls; as with united ascriptions of praise and thanksgiving they rendered homage to the Redeemer who had brought them safely out of the joys and sorrows of earth to the rest and joy of the heavenly temple ; they did not forget to bless again and again this house of God to which as lovers and friends, parents and children they had walked so often in company.

We would fain believe that on the present occasion a still larger assembly is present of the spirits who have gone before, some of whose faces and forms we have often seen in this house and cannot forget whenever we come here to worship. What looks of love do they cast upon us, what unseen glances of unspeakable tenderness and sympathy! What words do they breathe of unspoken affection, what prayers and praises do they present which we may not hear! With what homage do they regard this venerated sanctuary! What an estimate do they place upon the work which it has wrought! With tender and reverent care they commit it to the hands of the present generation, to alter and decorate it as they will, if it may better serve the needs of the present and the future, but charging us to retain if possible, even for another century, the house which has survived the first with such steady persistence, and served so many generations so well.

ADDRESSES.

ADDRESS OF Rev. SETH BLISS, BERLIN.

[For want of time a part of this was not spoken on the occasion.]

LADIES AND GENTLEMEN :

I am not a native of this town. An Irishman replied to the question where were you born? "I was born five miles from any place." Although I was born more than five miles from Farmington, I claim affinity with one of its pioneer settlers.

John Root emigrated from Gadby, England, and settled in this town in 1640. He was one of its founders, and also of the Church. A man of distinction and of good estate, he was one of the signers to the agreement for the settlement of the town as one of the original proprietors. My claim dates back to this sturdy Puritan ; for I married a Root of the seventh generation in the direct line of descent from him. I am happy to recognize in your Committee a gentleman in the same line of descent from John Root.* Doubtless there are others here sprung from this vigorous Root. His oldest son, Stephen, was a noted man, and called the giant of Farmington ; of strong build, standing six feet and six inches, of herculean strength, fearless courage, great energy, and inflexible will.

Foot-racing was one of the pastimes of that day. But one Indian was found who could outrun him. He beat every white man in town. So confident of his fleetness and power of endurance that he challenged one to the race, with an ox-chain around his own shoulders. No hostile Indian dared approach him, well knowing that a blow from his long arm would prostrate him ; and if one saw Stephen raising his long gun, unconditional surrender was the only hope of his life. If he turned to run he knew the unerring ball would crush through his back. He was engaged for two and a half years in wars with the Indians.

He was with Major Treat in the assault and capture of Fort Narragansett ; and it is said, that with his huge musket and sword did terrible execution. He belonged to the Cromwellian age, given to prayer, but careful to keep his powder dry. He was a prodigy in marches and campaigns, of "great mind and sound judgment." Himself and family united with this church. Had not this town and church sprung from such vigorous Roots this durable building and this intelligent community would not be here to-day. Let us on this occasion honor the heroic and self-sacrificing men that knew on what foundation to build for God,

---

* Hon. John S. Rice.

for the church, for the State and posterity. Their works do follow them, and
the next centennial will honor their memory. Is it not laudable to claim affinity
with such men? Permit me to say that for almost fifty years I have found myself *blissfully "rooted and grounded"* with one descended from one of the fathers
of this town and this church. Were not this so, probably I should not be here
at four-score years to join with you in these reminiscences, and perhaps her with
whom I am rooted would not in vigor have survived her seventy-sixth year. If
you should say to me as Paul said to the Jews at Rome, "boast not thyself; for
thou bearest not the Root, but the Root thee," I cheerfully submit. The question
is not debateable. Although a stranger to this generation, will you admit my
claim to affinity with all the good in Farmington?

I pass to another claim founded on ecclesiastical grounds.

Fifty years ago I resided here, and statedly worshiped in this temple for nearly
two years. From this pulpit I have been instructed, edified and comforted.
Within these walls I have witnessed scenes of momentous interest—God and
souls covenanting for time and eternity.

I must tell you how all this came to pass. The revival of religion which extensively blessed the churches of this State, and most abundantly this church in
1820 and 1821, commenced in the New Haven churches. Brethren from those
were invited to visit other churches and relate the origin and progress of that
revival. I was one of three who accepted the invitation to visit the First Church
in Hartford in the afternoon, and this church in the evening of the same day.
When we left Hartford a violent snow-storm had commenced. With difficulty
we reached here in time. Notice of the meeting was given on the previous Sabbath, and the people earnestly invited to hear us. The bell was to give notice of
our arrival.

The Holy Spirit was already preparing the way of the Lord. The notice of
the meeting and the earnest appeal of the pastor, had set many to thinking on
their spiritual state. What, said they, can those men tell us that we have not
often heard? They must believe that they can say something important for us
to hear and we will hear them." Let me give one illustration of this. General
George Cowles, a prominent citizen, was an early subject of the revival. Relat-
ing his experience, he said, "The notice of the meeting led me to think of my
religious state and prospects for eternity. This subject so engrossed my mind
that when the storm began I feared the brethren would not come and the meeting
fail. When the bell struck I was shaving. It so startled me that I dropped my
razor and sat down to collect my thoughts; for it seemed like a summons to the
final judgment." As was said in the discourse this morning, the Holy Spirit
came like a mighty rushing wind sweeping over the community.

Our meeting filled the hall, and closed with an urgent appeal from the pastor
to give immediate attention to the subject. On the next morning, two of the
deacons with the pastor, invited me to come here and pursue my studies, saying
there were no young men in the church to assist in religious meetings. Mr. Edward Hooker offered me a home in his family, and aid in study. Early in the
next week, February, 1821, I returned. The first enquiry meeting had been held
and filled a private parlor. The following week Mr. Nettleton came to the aid
of the pastor. No private room could now accommodate the numerous enquirers.
For successive weeks they filled the public hall. His preaching was searching,
stirring the conscience and quickening self-consciousness, revealing the sinner to

himself. Let me give one instance of this. The morning after he had preached in his most pungent manner, an excited hearer called on the pastor and intimated that he had given Mr. N. his private history. He was assured to the contrary, and that not even his name had been mentioned to him. To confirm this Mr. N. was called into the room and said to the man, "you must be mistaken, for no one has said a word to me respecting you." He at once discerned the cause of his trouble and closed the interview with prayer. That man was in the next enquiry meeting and there found peace. He is not here to-day, for he was then past middle life.

That beautiful June Sabbath referred to this morning, I well remember ; when 115 persons, husband and wife, parents and children, the aged, and the young thronged all these aisles with, morally speaking, the *élite* of the congregation, to covenant with God and this church for this world and the next.

Those who witnessed that scene never can forget it. Oh, that you could have witnessed the joy and gratitude of their faithful pastor, who, for sixteen years, had earnestly preached and prayed for such triumphs of divine truth and grace, and heard his jubilant sermon on that day, from Ps. 126 ; 1, 2, 3. He regarded that revival as an ever memorable era in the history of this ancient church, in not only adding largely to its members, but lifting it to a higher plane and a more vigorous life. Few of those who then stood in these aisles, and professed their love for the Lord Jesus Christ, and of those who filled these seats, are here to-day, and fewer still, probably, that recollect the speaker as a witness of that scene. They are gone—gone with their beloved pastor to adorn the crown of their Redeemer.

Let me in this connection speak of the eloquent Griffin referred to this morning, and whose voice has been heard from this pulpit, and recite an instance of his eloquence related to me by Dr. Porter.

After declining the call of this church, he settled in New Hartford. A powerful revival soon blessed the neighboring church of Torringford. The pastor, Father Mills, as we are accustomed to call him, invited the youthful Griffin to labor a week with him. On returning to his own charge he found himself so prostrated as to forbid his usual preparation for the Sabbath. Entering his pulpit he told the congregation that he was so exhausted by his labors in Torringford, he had no sermon for them, and that the best he could do was to relate some of the scenes he had witnessed there. At the close of his thrilling narrative he contrasted their low religious state with that of the Torringford church. He was himself so moved by the contrast, that his emotions choked his utterance and he sat down in tears. The people too were as deeply moved A wave of divine influence swept over the congregation. Tears flowed in the pews. The pulpit broke down, and then the pews broke down, and the people retired weeping and praying for help.

That was the beginning of the most powerful revival New Hartford had ever seen.

Those who have heard the matchless voice of that distinguished man and felt his great emotional power will readily account for such effects.

HERE let this house stand externally unchanged in its Puritan simplicity and strength, to the honor of God and its wise builders. HERE three generations have worshiped the Triune God. From this pulpit the blessed gospel of his Son has been faithfully proclaimed. HERE souls have been born of Heaven. HERE the weary and heavy laden sinner has found rest. HERE the children of

God have been edified, strengthened, and comforted in their sorrows. HERE thousands have commemorated the great sacrifice of Infinite Love. LET IT STAND, and transmit all these sacred associations to three coming generations more, who may successively worship within these walls, occupy these seats, learn the true way to happiness and heaven; that the sixth generation may celebrate its second centennial in renewing the sacred reminiscences of two centuries. As the years pass, one after another will rise from this temple to the eternal temple above, and there unite with the redeemed of all ages, and with the thousands born to a heavenly life here, in crowning Him LORD OF ALL whom they having not seen on earth yet loved. "As it was in the beginning, is now, and ever shall be," while earthly temples endure.

ADDRESS OF Hon. FRANCIS GILLETTE.

MR. CHAIRMAN, AND LADIES AND GENTLEMEN OF FARMINGTON:

I am happy to be here on this memorial occasion, to participate with you in its pleasant memories. My heart beats in glad unison with your hearts to the voices of the past, and the joys of the present. Although I cannot claim the honor of being a son of Farmington—only a son-in-law, which, I have reason to think, in my own case, at least, the better kind of sonship—I am deeply interested in whatever concerns her lineal sons; in all their bright memories of the past; their high aims of the present, and their sanguine hopes of the future. How could it be otherwise! With you sleep many dear ones—half of my own household, and others allied to me by many tender ties; and, though it was not my lot to begin the race of life with you, I anticipate ending it here, erelong, and resting sweetly from all its vicissitudes of good and ill, its hopes and fears, its joys and sorrows, in your own green and peaceful vale, lulled by the music of its gently flowing river.

When invited to say something on this occasion I promised to do so provided I could think of anything to say; for of all men, and women even, those who talk when they have nothing to say, are the most tedious and intolerable. To be of their number I should deem a great misfortune to myself, and a greater one to my audience.

Another source of apprehension which gave me some disquietude, after I had made the rash promise, was, that if any bright thoughts should come to bless me, other preceding speakers would anticipate me in giving them expression – as might be the case where many speak on the same theme—and thus leave me somewhat in the predicament of that Dutch author, who parried the charge of plagi-rism by accusing the thievish ancients of having stolen all his best thoughts.

But to come to the subject of my story; I have an additional word to say concerning this noble old meeting-house, whose first Centennial we celebrate to-day. I well remember the impression it gave me when, for the first time, I crossed its northern threshold, as a grateful worshiper on the Thanksgiving-day morning of 1834. Its quaint, tub-like, old pulpit, high above the pews, beneath which sat in awful gravity two most venerable deacons, and over which hung a pear-shaped canopy by a stem hardly visible, just ready to fall upon the head of the good

9

minister—all arrested my attention and excited speculation. As nearly as I can recollect the conclusion to which I came concerning the design or use of the wooden avalanche, was, that it was an invention, not to help the preacher's voice, which needed no help, but to hang over him *in terrorem*, after the manner of the sword of Damocles, to fall and crush him, should he preach any false doctrine. So it seemed a pulpit-extinguisher, or heresy-annihilator. It had a very Calvinistic look; dark, grim, and terrible. It was suggestive of the doctrine of decrees, or the Divine fore-ordination of whatsoever cometh to pass, which one of its devotees, in the olden time, of this place probably, though the story does not say so, illustrated in this wise: He used always to be saying to his wife and friends that they "should not take any trouble or anxiety about their lives, since the moment of their death was writ before the foundation of the world and they could not alter it. It was decreed, fore-ordained, unchangeable. It is as fixed as the throne of Heaven." This champion of the doctrine of decrees having occasion, one day, to pass over the frontier of the settlement into the Indian country, his good wife observed that he took the utmost pains in preparing his gun. He put in a new flint and new priming, taking every precaution to be prepared for the worst, should he meet a hostile Indian. As he was starting with his gun on his shoulder, fully accoutred, with powder-horn and shot-pouch hanging on either side, it seemed to his observant wife that his practice was not in keeping with his precept, and she said to him very blandly, as wives know how to do, "My dear, why do you take that gun? If it was writ before the foundation of the world, that you are to be killed by an Indian, on your journey, that gun won't prevent it; and if you are not to be killed, of course that gun is entirely unnecessary; so why do you take it at all?"

"Yes," he replied, "to be sure, my dear, of course you are right, perfectly right, and that is a very sensible and proper view; but see here, my dear, now—really—but—then—you see, my dear; to be sure—ahem—but supposing—supposing I should meet with a bloody Indian while I am gone, and *his* time had come, according as it was writ before the foundation of the world, and I hadn't my gun with me, what would he do? You never thought of that—did you? Remember, my dear, we must all do what we can to fulfil the decrees of Providence."

We infer the character of men from the works which they leave behind them. By their fruits ye shall know them. This house reveals the character and taste of its builders. In the first place, I notice the ample provision made in its architecture for the admission of light. If, as it is said, windows are the eyes of a house, surely this house can see wondrously well. It may be said to be Argus-eyed and more. Like the four beasts which St. John saw, it is full of eyes, before, behind, and on all sides. Obviously, its builders believed in the sun rather than in beautifully painted windows and candle-light. "The dim, religious light," spoken of by the poet, had no charms for them, as it struggles in scantily through discoloring windows and cuts up ridiculous shines on peoples' faces within. On the contrary, they practically agreed with Milton in his grand apostrophe to light:

> "Hail, holy light! offspring of heaven, first-born;
> Or of the eternal, co-eternal beam;
> Bright effluence of bright essence increate!"

No, no, the fathers had no partiality for Gothic cathedrals, with their darkened windows, uncouth images, ghostly pillars, and sepulchral dimness. Puritanism loved light rather than darkness, walked in the light, rejoiced in the light, and echoed the Divine command, Let there be light! Diogenes with his flickering torch at noon-day, searching through Athens for an honest man, was a type and forerunner of those modern church architects, who shut out the cheerful, all-animating sunlight, and take to gas and spermaceti. The builders of this house did not thus insult and dishonor the glorious king of day, and put darkness for light. I honor their memories as children of the light, and light-diffusers to the surrounding world.

Another characteristic of the architecture of this house, illustrative of the character of its builders, is, the great thoroughness with which it was built. There is nothing superficial or shammy about it. After a hundred years it is looking as fresh and beautiful to-day, with its royal garniture of flowers, as a bride adorned for her husband. Who would suppose that three generations have passed through it on their pilgrimage to eternity! Indeed, it promises well for another century or two, and possibly, possibly, the King of glory, at his second coming may find it here, and, as the good Shepherd, gather his lambs within its fold. Who can tell? It was built for the ages. No pains were spared to make it a worthy gift to posterity. It was founded upon a rock. Its timbers are massive oak; its covering is the selected mountain pine, and, though the winds and rains and wintry storms of a century have beaten upon it, it still stands firm, lifting its tall and graceful spire steadily toward the heaven whither so many of its humble worshipers have gone, and pointing us to the same blessed hereafter. May it stand forever. May floods of golden sunlight continue long to stream in through its many windows, and the higher light of life shine, as hitherto, brightly reflected from its pulpit. May generation after generation gather here before their Maker, and be illumined and safely guided through all these earthly labyrinths to their heavenly home. We welcome them to these seats and to this altar. We send down to them from this Centennial our cordial greetings and Christian salutations. We stretch out our eager hands to them with tender solicitude. We admonish them to be faithful to the God of their fathers, and true to their country. We bid them be of good courage and press on to that great victory which overcometh the world. We leave to them the standard of the Cross and the flag of Freedom, charging them, by the dear names of Immanuel and of Washington, to guard them well, and never surrender them, never dishonor them, never let them go down.

Much more presses to be spoken in commemoration of the illustrious builders of this house, and their contemporaries, but time would fail me to speak minutely of their many virtues. They were stern men, noble men, kingly men, positive men, who had convictions and courage to follow them. They were rocked in the cradle of the old Revolution, and believed, with all their might, in George Washington, and the Westminster Assembly's Catechism. Adversity was their nurse; hardship their ally. Shams and softness, laziness and prodigality they despised; truth and sincerity, industry and frugality, courage and honesty they loved. Like their own forest-oaks they stood firm, and gained strength and expansion from every passing storm. They could not be moved, for God was at their right hand. If their faith did not remove mountains, it surmounted them by triumphing over great difficulties and discouragements.

Rise, O my soul! survey the path
   By ancient worthies trod;
Aspiring, view those holy men
   Who lived and walked with God.
Though dead they speak in reason's ear,
   And in example live;
Their faith and hope and mighty deeds
   Still fresh instruction give.

REMARKS OF ELIHU BURRITT, LL. D., AT THE FARMINGTON CENTENARY, Oct. 16th.

There are no family gatherings that present such social aspects as those of a mother church and its children, and grandchildren. A single, private family often has but a transient life, or a temporary location. Its members scatter themselves through the country, and death or dispersion leaves the old homestead to fall into other hands. But a church is a family that never dies, never emigrates, never loses its local habitation or name. From century to century it preserves all the relations and characteristics of a single family. It always embraces in its social circle the old and young, men, women, and children. You never see a gray-haired church, nor one all in the summer locks of middle life, or one all in the golden hair of youth. Every village church embraces all these ages and aspects of life; and it is the only human family on earth that may be called immortal.

Then there is no building so social in its structure, object, and enjoyment as one of the old fashioned New England churches like this. The temples, palaces, and pyramids of the heathen world were all erected by compulsory or unrequited labor. The Christian religion is the only system of faith and sentiment that ever erected a public building on the perfectly voluntary and social principle. One hundred years ago, how this green and lovely valley, and these mountains that hold it in their arms, resounded with all the axes and hammers of the forefathers of the village at work upon this house of God! It was a father's house to them; it was to be the religious home of all their families blended into one happy and lasting fellowship. It was the unpaid work of love and faith. It was an honest work in every beam, and brace, and rafter. It was a home work from floor to ceiling, roof and steeple. Doubtless every nail fastened in a sure place was wrought on the village anvil. And what those early fathers built and gave to their children was received and treasured as a precious heir-loom by them. And many of us have come up from neighboring towns to thank them for preserving this religious home of their fathers up to this day in all the integrity of its original form and structure; and, for one, I hope it may thus stand for a hundred years to come. If it does not, it will not be its own fault; for there were giants in those days, and the mighty timbers they put into their church buildings were designed and able to last for centuries.

It is an honor to the people of this venerable mother town that they have preserved such a historical monument as this, even detached from its religious associations and objects. I do not know how many churches in this State have reached a hundred years on their original foundations. This is not only a historical monument, but a historical measure. If we put it against the past as such a measure, what comparisons does it make or suggest? This building was erected by the colonial subjects of the British crown. Its foundations were laid by men who had not seen one stone brought to the edifice of the American Union. These walls are ten years older than the structure of this great Continental Republic.

I have called Farmington a mother-town. So she is; so she has been, a kind and generous mother, for nearly two hundred years, to the communities she has begotten. She is the mother of full twelve tribes, who recognize that affectionate and maternal relation here to-day. And, to her honor and to their own be it said, that though she numbers as many children as Jacob could boast, not one of them has ever proved so indiscreet and unfortunate as his only daughter, Dinah. Not one of them ever made a clandestine or improper alliance with the aboriginal tribes who once possessed this goodly land, or even with the Dutch settlers on the Connecticut or Hudson, or with any other questionable Gentiles.

I feel it a great honor and privilege to say a few words on this happy occasion on behalf of one, if not the oldest daughter of our common mother. Of all the scattered members of her family that came up to worship at this common Jerusalem of their religious instruction and fellowship, New Britain, at least, had the longest and hardest miles to travel. For none of the rest had such hills and mountains to cross as the families of "Ye Great Swamp," as our ambitious town was then called. To children this was an immense and laborious distance. Every one must know that when there are only six inches between a boy's knee and the sole of his foot, the miles are very long and the houses and hills very high. I remember well this experience of heights, depths, and lengths on this very mountain road. For when I made my first journey to Farmington, I stepped off the whole distance with a pair of legs not much longer than those of a carpenter's compass. New Britain at that time was smaller still, compared with its present size, than I was compared with a full-grown man. On the whole site of our city there were hardly a dozen dwelling-houses to be seen, and these were of very ordinary structure and aspect. I never shall forget the feeling of awe and admiration which the first sight of Farmington produced in my child's mind. After the longest walk I had ever made on my small bare feet, we came suddenly upon the view of this glorious valley and of the largest city I had ever conceived of. I was smitten with wonder. I dared not go any farther, though urged by my older brothers. I clambered up the Sunset Rock, and sitting down on the edge with my feet over the side, looked off upon the scene with a feeling like that of a man first coming in view of Rome and its St. Peters. I had never before seen a church with a steeple, and measuring this above us with a child's eye it seemed to reach into the very heavens. This steeple crowned all the wonders I saw. I sat and gazed at it until my brothers returned to me. And this thought was uppermost in all that filled my mind. I remember it as if it were the thought of yesterday. If I could only stand where that brass rooster stood on the steeple, could I not look right into heaven and see what was going on there? Or if that were a live rooster, and should crow every morning, could not all the good Farmington people who had gone to heaven, hear him, and know by his voice that he was a Farmington rooster, and would they not all be glad to hear him crow, not only that they were so happy, but because so many of their children were safely on the way to the same happiness. In later years I learned that what to my youthful imagination appeared to be a rooster was in fact a crown, placed there in honor of the king under whose reign this house was erected, which was subsequently changed to a star, as it is at the present time.

This was the honest, reverent thought of a child, at his first sight of this church. And now the same child having become a man, and having seen a good many taller steeples even than this, it is a great pleasure to me to stand within these walls as a member of one of the religious communities represented here today, and to share with them the hallowed associations and memories which this anniversary is so calculated to revive. It is one of the happy experiences of this occasion, that we have had the distinguished privilege of listening to the history of this church and community from the lips of a son whom Farmington holds in a pride and affection which we all share, not only by birthright inheritance, but by those higher affinities and relationships which have impressed his name and character upon the intellectual history, progress, and moral stature of the American nation.

REMARKS BY LEVERETT GRIGGS,
Late Pastor of the Congregational church in Bristol.

This house an hundred years old! These walls, roof, and even the shingles! I have often stated this fact, but could hardly credit my own statement. Last week I met with a Farmington man and had my faith reassured; now I believe it is really so. This frame is all just as massive and firm as when first erected, and the whole structure is more beautiful than on the day of its dedication, for it has some adornments without and within such as it did not originally possess. It is like an aged matron who is matured in wisdom, and mellowed by piety, and thus rendered more dignified and lovely than in early youth.

We have come from Bristol to pay our filial tribute of veneration and love to this mother of churches. We derived our life from this parent stock, and for years it was sustained by supplies from the same source. In fact Bristol was once a part of Farmington, as were several other neighboring towns. The first deed ever made in our section, was given to a man from this place in 1727. So likewise the second. From that period the settlers multiplied, but came to this center for Sabbath worship and religious privileges the year round till 1742. Then the Legislature allowed them to establish and maintain public worship by themselves six months in the year. Hence that portion of the town was called the " Winter Parish," or " South West Society," and afterward "New Cambridge" when they were incorporated an Ecclesiastical Society. During all those years till 1747 they depended on this church for the enjoyment of Christian ordinances.

That year—1747—the church in Bristol was organized, and the first minister settled. And whence did he come? From Southington, which was only a part of Farmington. If he be not acknowledged as one of your offspring, surely the "better half" of him will be, for his wife was one of your own refined and polished daughters. She was the widow of Mr. Timothy Root. Her first name was Mary Hart. And after the Rev. Samuel Newell passed away, at the close of his forty-two years' pastorate, who was his successor? The Rev. Giles Hooker Cowles. He was one of your sons of course, for who ever heard of a Cowles that was not born in Farmington, or could not easily trace his lineage to this ancient home? The excellent wife of our sixth pastor was also from this place —Mrs. Catharine L. Seeley, daughter of Hon. Timothy Cowles. Thus it appears that two ministers and two ministers' wives were furnished by this mother for the church in Bristol.

Moreover, from time to time we have been indebted to this same source for many of our most exemplary members. Some of them were born and reared among you; others, though they originated in other places, were here "born again" and afterward became pillars in our Zion. Thus we make our acknowledgements for your forming and fostering influence which pervades all our history.

I cannot close without a word respecting him who ministered to you more than half a century in this sacred place. I enjoyed a partial acquaintance with him for many years, as his eldest son was one of my honored college class-mates. After I came into this neighborhood my knowledge of Dr. Porter became more familiar and intimate. I learned not only to venerate, but also admire and love him, for he was one of the most wise and holy men I ever knew.

As you review the last century you find much to fill you with delight. You may well be proud of your ancestors and proud of your sons; and as we contemplate the life and labors of the holy men and women who have gone before, let us all be " followers of them who through faith and patience inherit the promises."

Rev. Mr. FESSENDEN
Spoke substantially as follows:

Mr. Chairman:

I hoped not to have been called upon at this late hour and in the presence of so many strangers from whom we should be glad to hear. But in answer to your call I will say a few words in behalf of this community.

We are happy to welcome here to-day so many who trace their parentage to this community, or who represent the churches and congregations which have sprung from this venerable mother church. We rejoice and cherish a paternal pride in them. We thank God for their number and prosperity, their steadfastness in the faith and their great usefulness. We shall ever pray for God's continued blessing upon them.

Allow me to express the great satisfaction with which we listened to the very able, interesting, and appropriate address of Pres. Porter this morning. It was a most becoming tribute to an honored ancestry. It was all that we desired, and will possess a historic value not easily over-estimated. This, Sir, adds another to the many, and great obligations which this community owe to the Porter family. We are not unmindful of, nor insensible to, them.

It was in the fall of 1838, thirty-four years ago, that I first became acquainted with Farmington. It was then my delightful privilege to spend a few days in the family of the ever loved and revered Dr. Porter; and on Thanksgiving day and the following Sabbath for the first time to listen to his pulpit exercises. I can never forget the impression then made upon me and which was many times repeated by them in after years. Every thing in the appearance, the manner, and the utterances of this venerable servant of God was becoming the solemnity of the place and the occasion. There was great simplicity, seriousness, and appropriateness. His invocations and prayers were the natural expressions of a true shepherd, and spiritual leader and guide, receiving their characters and a special pertinency from the circumstances of his flock and their special conditions and wants. His sermons were uniformly of a very high order. They were eminently practical discussions of just those subjects which were adapted to instruct, convert, edify, and comfort his hearers. They at different times covered a wide range of topics, and illustrated and enforced them with great copiousness and variety of thought, with great logical force, and, not unfrequently, with remarkable beauty and elegance of style and imagery. Generally they were confined closely to a single topic. It was naturally drawn from the text, and was usually formally stated. It stood forth in bold relief throughout the discourse. The speaker was soon lost in his subject. The interest of every thoughtful and attentive hearer was secured, and increased as the speaker advanced; and it was not uncommon for the whole audience to be hushed to stillness and sometimes to be greatly moved by the convincing, and persuasive, and powerful exhibitions of truth thus made. It was by such a ministry of the gospel of Christ, during a period of more than 50 years, that manifold and inestimable blessings were secured to this people.

On the afternoon of that Sabbath day I for the first time officiated in that pulpit. A remarkable and most interesting spectacle was presented by the congregation before me. It was before the congregations of Plainville and Unionville were formed, and a large number of the people of those villages were accustomed statedly to worship in this house, which was often filled full. I recall the appearance of many of the aged men and women of the congregation, some of whom usually occupied the pews directly in front of the pulpit. There were the Lewis's, and Crampton's, the Thompson's and Gays, the Stanley's, and Langdon's. In yonder seat was the tall and courtly figure of Gen. Solomon Cowles. Behind him was the stalwart frame and noble countenance of Major Timothy Cowles,— next to him sat the late Mr. John T. Norton, a noble example of a true New England man. Having early acquired a competence in Albany, by his integrity, industry, and business skill, he in mid life returned to his native town and built a beautiful home near the spot of his birth. There the later years of his life were passed, devoted to the pursuits of agriculture, in the quiet and culture of a beloved family, the friend and patron of everything good. Yonder was the seat of the sagacious and staunch Horace Cowles, and near him the peace loving, and peace making Edward Hooker. There was the beloved physician, Asahel Thompson, and there the benevolent, and eminently useful and successful teacher, Dea. Simeon Hart. These and other scarcely less remarkable men then gave character to this community. They were strong minded, God fearing, ho est men, who carried their religion with them into all the walks of life; and having faithfully served God and their fellow-men in their day and generation, one .. ter another they have passed away. Do you wonder that their children cherish their memories, and honor their virtues, and are so richly blessed in their inheritance?

In closing, let me say that those who now occupy the places of such an ancestry are not unmindful of the high responsibilities devolved upon them. They desire to transmit this priceless heritage to those who shall come after them. We love this sacred place and the church which still lives and worships within these walls. We desire that the precious truths on which this church was founded shall here ever be taught and preached. Our prayer and effort shall be that we may never prove recreant to the high and sacred trust which God has devolved upon us.

ISAAC G. PORTER, M. D.,

of New London, being called upon, responded, substantially as follows:

After a ride of seventy miles, in honor of this occasion, I find myself once more at the shrine of this dear old church, erected, in part, by and for my ancestors, and in a town where the early and forming period of my life was spent. My father used to say to me, with a twinkle in his eye, "I helped build that church." "But how so," said I, "when you were born as late as 1765?" In reply he said: "When the heavy beams and rafters were raised, I pulled at the end of the ropes." But my "right and title" here are more direct, since my grandfather, then forty years of age, doubtless, did a yeoman's service at the raising, and my great-grandfather, then seventy-five years of age, sat within its walls for ten years, before he exchanged an earthly temple for an heavenly.

Surrounded as I am by familiar objects, yet unfamiliar faces, the spirit of Hood's impressive lines comes over me:

> "I remember, I remember
> The house where I was born,
> The little window, where the sun
> Came peeping in at morn."

So, associated with these surroundings, I live over again the sports of youth, and particularly, just now, the pastime of visiting the old belfry, whenever, *fas aut nefas*, I could gain access. With some, perhaps, of the reflections of Cowper's "Jackdaw in the church steeple," it was pleasant to witness the circling flight of the swallows, whose dominion we had invaded, but without disturbing their nests beneath the eaves. Thus was explained the longing psalmist's imagery: "the sparrow hath found an house, and the swallow a nest for herself where she may lay her young, even thine altars, O Lord of Hosts, my king and my God." Wherever I have been situated, on the land or on the sea, if by any process, this text is suggested, my mind immediately reverts to these youthful experiences. I use the words, as you perceive, *"fas aut nefas,"* "right or wrong," for the mention of the belfry and the thought of the bell-rope brings another incident to my mind. Some of the elder inhabitants may remember our rather fee' and old sexton, Daniel Pratt. Though of the same name, he is not *the peripatetic*, but a worthier man, because he served his generation with the ability, however small, which God had given. The incident, very properly, perhaps, suggests to me the propriety of the psalmist's prayer: " Remember not, O Lord, the sins of my youth." But the associations of the moment bring to mind how the boys of the period used to delight in thwarting his best concerted plans for preventing our entrance into the church, or belfry, on week-days. He was once at work, remote from the church, when a few strokes of the bell, at intervals, informed him of the success of our strategy. After a time, the vidette stationed on the square stair in the porch, announced his approach on a slow run. We kept the bell in motion, until just as his key entered the back door, when we scattered in all directions, but not until we heard him say : " you had better scamper, you young rascals, ringing fire-bell here for half an hour." Will some one say : " this is beneath the dignity of the occasion ?" But is not a little pleasantry allowable in the last speech when all are anxious to depart? Besides, was not " uncle Daniel " a *character* and entitled to notice, on the ground of having been " doorkeeper of this house of the Lord " or, at least, the keeper of its keys ? I was once reading at home, Blair's poem, " The Grave," when he came in. Says I to him : " Uncle Daniel, here is something for you. This poem is on the subject of the grave and the author says, speaking of the sexton,

"And soon, some trusty brother of the trade
Must do for him what he has done for thousands."

It struck him forcibly, for he remarked : " Now that is right to the point—and it's true too."

You may think that this was *grave* reading for a lad. Perhaps it was so ; but in those days, books were scarce. My sabbath hours were often whiled away in looking over the pages of the Connecticut Evangelical Magazine, or the Panoplist, or Burder's Village Sermons. Then, we had no literary lectures, certainly none on a "Course of Reading," for the means of carrying out its suggestions were not to be found in the " Farmington Monthly Library " even if supplemented by the " Phœnix."

But I remember other and less frivolous matters. Before the era of Sabbath Schools, and as their substitute and forerunner, the youth were accustomed to assemble in the square pews, on Saturday afternoons, to recite the Assembly's Catechism. As a type, or example, of the influences, which proceeded from that pulpit, I may refer to a sermon preached by a returned missionary, during which, a veritable heathen idol was exhibited. It was a fact so realistic and palpable, that it made a lasting impression upon the minds of the young and contributed much towards the formation of a missionary spirit among us. Its fruits have doubtless multiplied and been felt on other continents and the islands of the sea. As an early result, a missionary garden was cultivated among us, producing among other things a good crop of radishes, which were sent by stage to Litchfield, much as our wants are now supplied by the warmer climes of Norfolk or Charleston.

But I must acknowledge, with gratitude, the happy, religious and educational influences which were exerted by that pulpit, with its choice language, its rational methods of thought, and its words of wisdom. I remember a sermon preached in my early youth by Rev. Dr. Hawes, of Hartford, on the text, "And Enoch walked with God and was not, for God took him." A spiritual atmosphere at the time may have pervaded the people—for it was long remembered by those who heard it and its influences may have culminated in the powerful revival which soon after followed. These, it is true, are but the experiences of a single mind, but let them be multiplied by the number of hearers, and who can tell the possible influence.

Doubtless, some may remember, with me, the time when our front gallery was occupied by a company of ladies in caps and spectacles. Their voices, unlike wine and friendship, may not have improved with age, but the object to be attained, so honorable to their kindness of heart, was of sufficient interest and importance to draw out all who had the reputation of being good singers. A choir was thus formed, with "the beloved physician," Dr. Eli Todd, as their leader, thus securing his attendance at the house of God; and there is reason to believe, that like other truly benevolent efforts, its influence was not fruitless, the buried seed ultimately springing into spiritual life.

Forty years since, at the outset of active professional life, I attended worship for a single day, in this church, since which time, if my memory serves me, I have never entered it. Personally, the fact is interesting. In retrospect, what a vista, with its well-defined outlines, is presented! I, this morning, visited the mountain on the east, the same so graphically alluded to by Hon. Mr. Burritt, as the terminus of his youthful walk from New Britain. The vale which so entranced his vision, with the mountain beyond, lay outstretched before me, almost a Tempe for beauty. From a similar stand-point, mentally, I look over to the high table-lands of youth, the pilgrimage of life, its hopes and fears, its successes and disappointments occupying the valley between. As I return once more to duty and leave these dear old walls, probably for the last time, I bid them farewell! as to a living, conscious friend. If I ever reach the better land, I think I shall often re-visit this spot, the center of precious memories and the source and medium of blessed hopes.